barefoot
contessa
how easy is that?

barefoot contessa
how easy is that?

fabulous recipes & easy tips

ina garten

Photographs by Quentin Bacon

Clarkson Potter/Publishers
New York

Copyright © 2010 by Ina Garten

All rights reserved.
Published in the United States by Clarkson Potter/Publishers, an
imprint of the Crown Publishing Group, a division of Random
House, Inc., New York.
www.crownpublishing.com
www.clarksonpotter.com

CLARKSON POTTER is a trademark and POTTER with colophon is a
registered trademark of Random House, Inc.

Library of Congress Cataloging-in-Publication Data
Garten, Ina
    Barefoot Contessa, how easy is that? / Ina Garten. — 1st ed.
        p.   cm.
    Includes index.
    1. Cookery.   2. Barefoot Contessa (Store)   I. Title.
II. Title: How easy is that?
    TX714.G36445   2010
    641.5—dc22   2010002025

ISBN 978-0-307-23876-4

Printed in China

10 9 8 7 6 5 4 3 2

First Edition

For Jeffrey, who makes my
life fun—and so easy!

contents

thanks!

When I first started writing cookbooks I was terrified that it would be a very solitary existence; I'd be working by myself testing recipes at home in my kitchen. How could I be so wrong?? It turns out that writing cookbooks, which is the thing I love doing most, is a collaboration with some of the most extraordinarily creative people I've ever known. And the best part is that I love working with them. My kitchen is like a big sandbox—there's always something interesting to do there and it's filled with my friends. How great is that?

First is my wonderful assistant, Barbara Libath, who works side by side with me. I couldn't have done any of this without her and she makes every day like a "playdate." Second is my friend Sarah Chase, who writes amazing cookbooks and constantly inspires me with her creative ideas and recipes.

There's also a team of fabulous people who produce the photographs for my books—and I adore them all. Quentin Bacon is the most brilliant photographer, Cyd McDowell styles the delicious food, and Robert Rufino brings all the gorgeous props for us to play with. I love working with you all and I love our collaboration. Thank you also to Crate & Barrel for their generosity with their beautiful tableware, which we love to use.

There's also a fabulous team of publishers and editors who are incredibly inspiring—Jenny Frost, the former president of the Crown Publishing Group; Lauren Shakely, the publisher of Clarkson Potter; my editor, Rica Allannic; my book designer, Marysarah Quinn; my publicists, Amelia Durand and Kate Tyler; and the whole team of people who produce and market my cookbooks. Thank you all so much for your trust and support and for producing the most beautiful cookbooks possible.

Finally, my agent, Esther Newberg, who always believes in me and takes care of business so I can spend my time doing the fun stuff—writing cookbooks. And of course my husband, Jeffrey, without whose unconditional love I couldn't get through the day.

introduction

I get enormous pleasure from cooking and entertaining, but as much as I love good food and recipes that have interesting, complex flavors, there are two real secrets to my cooking. First, probably like you, I'm not a trained professional chef so the recipes need to be easy enough for me to make. Second, I have a very short attention span, and if a recipe goes on for pages and pages, using lots of complicated techniques and special equipment—forget about it! (If anyone asked me to make spun sugar, I'd have a meltdown!) When you get right down to it, I cook pretty much the same way you do; it's just that after thirty years in the food business, I may have a little more experience.

Frankly, all of us are so busy these days with jobs, families, friends, and houses to take care of that we don't really have the luxury of cooking all day anymore, and even if we did, who would want to?? Personally, I'm good for about two hours making a dinner party and thirty minutes for a weeknight meal; more than that and I have better things to do. But I'm still not willing to sacrifice any of the pleasure of making a delicious dinner for my husband, Jeffrey, and my friends.

This book is all about saving you time and avoiding stress.

This book is all about saving you time and avoiding stress. These aren't recipes with three ingredients that you can throw together in five minutes before dinner. These are tried-and-true Barefoot Contessa recipes that are easy enough to make but still have all that deep, delicious flavor that makes a meal so satisfying. I've tested the recipes endlessly, so I know they work; I've anticipated the kinds of problems you might encounter at home—and I've solved them before the recipe even gets into the book. These are recipes you'll make over and over again and you'll feel confident that they'll turn out perfectly every time. If you think that's easy, it's not!

easy ingredients

First, it starts with simple ingredients. I always ask myself, "Does every ingredient earn its place in this recipe?" If I can't clearly distinguish it or it

doesn't enhance the flavor of another ingredient, out it goes. Fewer ingredients mean less shopping and less prep time. Second, are they ingredients that you can easily find in a grocery or specialty food store? There's no point in writing a simple recipe if it means you have to go to three different produce markets to find three different kinds of wild mushrooms in order to make the recipe. I've seen recipes that call for gelatin sheets (where do you find those, except in a restaurant kitchen?) or a teaspoon of glace de viande. When I see ingredients like that in a recipe, I just put the book back on the shelf.

Instead, I love recipes with ingredients you can find in any well-stocked grocery store and that are called for in the quantities they come in. If canned tomatoes generally come in 28-ounce cans, you won't find a recipe of mine that calls for 32 ounces of canned tomatoes. What exactly are you supposed to do with the rest of the can? When I call for 9 ounces of Major Grey's chutney, you know when you find a 9-ounce jar, you've got exactly the right chutney. My Strawberry Shortcakes, Deconstructed (page 224) calls for 2 pints of fresh strawberries, which is exactly how you'll find them packed at the store. You also won't find recipes in my books that call for 2 teaspoons each of three different flavored vodkas so that you've spent a fortune and ended up with a shelf full of expensive liquor you'll never use again.

easy shortcuts

The next thing I look for is a way to take shortcuts that make a recipe even easier without losing all the great flavor. For my Rich Beef Barley Soup (page 58), instead of making beef stock from scratch, I start with canned beef broth and cook the soup with lots of inexpensive oxtails. It's one step instead of two and you'd never know that I didn't spend hours roasting beef bones in the oven! Spanish onions are twice as big as yellow onions so they're easier to handle and faster to chop. When a recipe calls for two onions, I often use one Spanish onion instead. Shortcuts like these just make cooking easier.

easy techniques

You also won't find a lot of recipes in my books for food that is sautéed, stir-fried, or made by other labor-intensive techniques. For me, the easiest thing is to throw something in the oven, set a timer, and forget about it. Grilling is great—and I've certainly done a lot of grilling—but it means you have to stand over a hot grill, away from everything else going on in the kitchen. The coals are too hot; they're too cold; you never really know when the food is done just right. Instead, my Steakhouse Steaks (page 138) are seared in a

cast-iron pan on the top of the stove and then thrown in the oven, the way restaurants make them. The steaks come out perfectly every time—seared on the outside, done to juicy perfection on the inside.

Or take French Toast Bread Pudding (page 20), the perfect example of making something easier. Instead of standing at the stove making French toast two slices at a time, I decided to combine all the ingredients of my challah French toast recipe in one baking dish and make it into a bread pudding. Same breakfast—but so easy! Out of the oven, a dusting of confectioners' sugar, a drizzle of maple syrup, and breakfast is ready for a crowd.

I love risotto as much as anyone but I hate standing at the stove for twenty-five minutes stirring and adding stock in small quantities. For my Easy Parmesan "Risotto" (page 160) you simply throw the rice and stock into a Dutch oven and put it in the oven. Forty-five minutes later, you stir

in the Parmesan and wine and serve up the most delicious risotto, lots of flavor—no stress. Meatballs and spaghetti are a great old-fashioned meal but I hate rolling all those meatballs around in a pan of hot fat—and then you have to clean yourself, the stove, and the ceiling. My Spicy Turkey Meatballs & Spaghetti (page 158) are made lighter with ground turkey and they're baked in the oven. And believe me, they're even more delicious than your grandmother's!

easy menus

Weeknight dinners are usually easier because I can make one or two things and dinner's ready. But dinner parties are a whole other thing; we all feel that we need to make something really special for our friends. Even with all my books full of easy recipes to make, though, my stress level can skyrocket if I try to cook six things at three different temperatures that all have to be done ten minutes before dinner. Instead, I make a plan: I'll stagger the work and the cooking times with recipes that work for me. With cocktails I'll serve Savory Coeur à la Crème (page 48)—a delicious cheese appetizer served with mango chutney and whole-grain crackers—which actually needs to sit overnight in the refrigerator, so it's ready whenever my guests arrive. Or I'll make my Roasted Eggplant Caponata (page 38), which tastes even better the next day. All I have to do is toast some pita bread in the oven and it's ready to serve. For dinner, I'll

choose an entrée like Caesar-Roasted Swordfish (page 150) so I can prepare the Caesar sauce early, slather it on the swordfish before dinner, and
bake it while we're sitting around having drinks. For a side dish, I'll make
Scalloped Tomatoes (page 170)—it's like a crusty tomato gratin—that I
can assemble early in the day and just throw into the oven before dinner.
By the time we're ready to eat, I'm not red in the face and completely
frazzled from running back and forth from the kitchen to the living room;
I'm relaxed and ready to have fun with my friends.

I really do keep the party menus pretty simple.
Your friends have come to see you—not to critique
your cooking skills! I'm asked all the time, "How
many hors d'oeuvres do I need to make before
dinner?" "None!" is my answer. If I've planned a
really good dinner for friends and it's going to take
more than two hours to prepare, I'll almost never
make hors d'oeuvres, unless they're really simple
like my Stilton & Walnut Crackers (page 43),
which I can freeze weeks ahead of time and
defrost, slice, and bake before dinner. Cocktail
food at my house is little silver bowls with salted
cashews, ripe cherry tomatoes, vinegary caperber-
ries, or salty potato chips. It's elegant, it's delicious,
and frankly, no one really wants to fill up on pigs
in blankets before a dinner that you've worked so
hard on.

For dessert, if I've already got three or four things to make for dinner,
I'll buy a few delicious treats to serve "as is"—I might get farmstand apples,
good English Cheddar, and some chilled hard apple cider; for a celebratory
dessert, I like long-stemmed strawberries dipped in chocolate, a glass of
demi-sec Champagne, and some store-bought cookies. And you probably
have a good bakery nearby that makes a special chocolate cake that everyone loves. Who wouldn't want that for dessert with some good vanilla ice
cream or fresh berries? You've served a really special dessert—and you
didn't even have to turn on the oven!

easy recipes

When I'm working on my cookbooks, I test the recipes over and over again—and then I hand them to my wonderful assistant, Barbara Libath, and watch her make them. Every time I do that, I learn something about how someone at home, with only the printed recipe in front of them, might make the dish. For example, when I worked on the recipe for Scalloped Tomatoes (page 170), the tomatoes need to sauté in a large pan for about five minutes. Barbara cut them and tossed them into the pan as she was cutting. Well, it took her about five minutes to cut the tomatoes, so the first tomatoes in the pan were overcooked and the last ones weren't done enough. Right there, I changed the instructions to cut the tomatoes into a bowl and add them to the pan all at once. Disaster averted!

I know it's easy to make a batch of perfect Red Velvet Cupcakes (page 218) if all you've got to do that day is make cupcakes. But are those cupcakes easy enough to prepare if you have four other things to make? I want to know the answers before the recipe goes into the book.

And finally, I "road-test" each and every one of these recipes on my own friends, so I know everyone loves the dish before it even gets into this book. When you make these dishes for your friends, you don't have to worry for a second. But I also want to know if everyone loves those Red Velvet Cupcakes. My friends did! And hopefully yours will, too. So, when I say, "Have fun!" I really mean it. If you make these recipes for your family and friends, not only will they have fun, but I promise, you will, too.

Have fun!

french toast bread pudding

SERVES 8

Each recipe in this book is designed to save you time and reduce stress when you cook. This is a good example. I was making Challah French Toast one morning from my Barefoot Contessa Family Style cookbook when I realized that the ingredients were exactly like a bread pudding—so I threw them all together in one dish and baked it. French Toast Bread Pudding for breakfast— all the flavor of French toast and none of the stress. How easy is that?

1	challah loaf, sliced ¾ inch thick (see note)
8	extra-large eggs
5 cups	half-and-half or milk
3 tablespoons	honey
1 tablespoon	grated orange zest
1 teaspoon	pure vanilla extract
¼ teaspoon	kosher salt
	Confectioners' sugar and pure maple syrup, for serving

Preheat the oven to 350 degrees.

Arrange the bread in two layers in a 9 × 13 × 2-inch baking dish, cutting the bread to fit the dish. Set aside.

In a large bowl, whisk together the eggs, half-and-half, honey, orange zest, vanilla, and salt. Pour the mixture over the bread and press the bread down. Allow to soak for 10 minutes.

Place the baking dish in a larger roasting pan and add enough very hot tap water to the roasting pan to come an inch up the side of the baking dish. Cover the roasting pan tightly with aluminum foil, tenting it so the foil doesn't touch the pudding. Make two slashes in the foil to allow steam to escape. Bake for 45 minutes, remove the aluminum foil, and bake for another 40 to 45 minutes, until the pudding puffs up and the custard is set. Remove from the oven and cool slightly.

With a small sieve, dust lightly with confectioners' sugar and serve hot in squares with maple syrup on the side.

If the challah is fresh, not stale, slice and bake for 10 minutes at 350 degrees.

68 easy tips

Like a good surgeon with the right scalpel, every good cook needs the right piece of equipment for each task. I hate specialized equipment—there's no need for a garlic press if the chef's knife you already own does the same job. However, you can't make thin slices of smoked salmon with a paring knife no matter how hard you try, and an

Parchment for
Sheet pans

Cook's Illustrated

extra bowl for your food processor is inexpensive and it means you only have to wash it half as many times while you're cooking. I've compiled dozens of tips throughout this book with things that have made cooking and entertaining *so* much easier for me. I hope you find some that you love, too!

Graduated glass bowls

Baking mixes

cocktails

pink grapefruit margaritas, page 37

watermelon mojitos

roasted figs & prosciutto

chunky blue cheese & yogurt dip

truffled popcorn

chipotle & rosemary roasted nuts

pink grapefruit margaritas

roasted eggplant caponata

smoked salmon deviled eggs

stilton & walnut crackers

grilled bread with prosciutto

crostini with tuna tapenade

savory coeur à la crème

5

Olio Santo Oil

6

Spice drawer

well-stocked pantry

Even with all the great recipes in the world, cooking will never truly be easy if you don't have a well-stocked pantry, refrigerator, and freezer. Nothing is more annoying than having to run out to the store—maybe more than once—in the middle of cooking because you forgot to check whether you had olive oil in the house. It's not that I have a million kinds of olive oil on my shelf; in fact, I only have one. But I make sure it's Olio Santo, a delicious all-purpose California olive oil that's good for cooking, for salad dressings, and as a dip for bread. I always make sure I have De Cecco pasta in lots of shapes, good San Marzano canned tomatoes, lots of different dried beans and grains, Hellmann's mayonnaise, Heinz ketchup, plus all the common baking supplies like all-purpose flour, sugars, baking powder, raisins, and nuts. My spice drawer is organized so I can always see what I have and what I need to buy—and I can put my hands on each spice without turning the drawer upside down! My freezer is stocked with a few important ingredients that I use all the time: homemade chicken stock, white truffle butter, sliced white bread, puff pastry, and vanilla ice cream. The refrigerator always has a big chunk of aged Parmigiano-Reggiano cheese, butter, eggs, milk, and Greek yogurt.

Since I use the same ingredients over and over again, with this relatively short list of items stocked, I know I won't have to shop for everything I need every time I cook. When it's time to make dinner, all I have to do is stop at the store and pick up a few perishables, like fresh salmon, fresh herbs, and a vegetable. Maintaining a well-stocked pantry is a habit I got into early in my cooking career and it makes my life so much easier.

watermelon mojitos

MAKES 6 DRINKS

Most cocktail recipes are written to make one drink at a time, but who has time for that when you're having a party? In the summer, when the watermelon is sweet, this recipe makes a big pitcher of mojitos—it's a refreshing drink with crushed mint and freshly squeezed lime juice.

30	large fresh mint leaves, coarsely torn by hand
3 to 4	thick slices fresh watermelon
12 ounces	light rum, such as Bacardi
½ cup	simple syrup (see note)
6 tablespoons	freshly squeezed lime juice (3 limes)
	Sprigs of mint and spears of watermelon, for serving

Use a mortar and pestle to mash the mint leaves. Remove and discard the rind and seeds of the watermelon. Put the fruit into a food processor fitted with the steel blade and purée. Put the mashed mint into a large pitcher with 2 cups of puréed watermelon, the rum, simple syrup, and lime juice and stir to combine. Pour the mixture into a pitcher for serving.

Place ice cubes in 6 glasses and pour the mojito mixture into the glasses. Garnish with sprigs of fresh mint and spears of watermelon. Serve ice cold.

To make simple syrup, put 1 cup sugar and 1 cup water in a small pan and simmer until the sugar dissolves. Chill.

roasted figs & prosciutto

SERVES 10

When figs are ripe, all you need to do is wrap them in prosciutto to enjoy them. However, I can almost never find really ripe figs in the market. Roasting figs concentrates the sugars in the fruit and brings out their sweetness—and heightens the salty/sweet contrast with the prosciutto. I assemble these early and throw them in the oven before guests arrive.

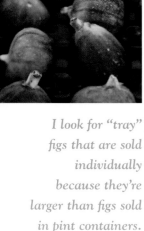

I look for "tray" figs that are sold individually because they're larger than figs sold in pint containers.

20   large fresh ripe figs (see note)
20   thin slices Italian prosciutto (about 8 ounces)
      Good olive oil

Preheat the oven to 425 degrees.

Snip the hard stems off the figs and cut the figs in half lengthwise through the stem. With a small sharp knife, cut the prosciutto lengthwise into inch-wide strips. Wrap a strip of prosciutto around the center of each fig half, with the ends overlapping. Brush with olive oil and arrange cut side up on a sheet pan.

Roast the figs for 10 minutes, until the prosciutto is a little crisp and the figs are warmed through. Serve warm.

chunky blue cheese
& yogurt dip

MAKES 2 CUPS

I love blue cheese dip but it's so rich when it's made with mayonnaise and sour cream. I thin the Italian Gorgonzola with some Greek yogurt and it's not only lighter but has an added tang of the yogurt. I serve this arranged on a big platter surrounded with crudités or crackers.

¼ cup	finely chopped shallot
1 teaspoon	minced garlic
2 tablespoons	freshly squeezed lemon juice
7 ounces	Greek-style yogurt, such as Fage Total
½ cup	good mayonnaise, such as Hellmann's
4 ounces	sharp (mountain) Gorgonzola, crumbled
5 dashes	Tabasco sauce, or to taste
1 teaspoon	kosher salt
½ teaspoon	freshly ground black pepper
3 tablespoons	minced fresh chives
	Crudités and/or crackers, for serving

Place the shallot, garlic, lemon juice, yogurt, mayonnaise, Gorgonzola, Tabasco, salt, and pepper in the bowl of a food processor fitted with the steel blade. Pulse the processor about 12 times, until the mixture is almost smooth but still a bit chunky. Add the chives and pulse two or three times, until combined. Transfer to a serving bowl, cover with plastic wrap, and chill for at least 2 hours to allow the flavors to develop. Serve with vegetables and/or crackers for dipping.

truffled popcorn

I love things that are highbrow and lowbrow at the same time, like potatoes with caviar. Dan Mathieu, a caterer in Boston, told me he makes truffled popcorn for parties and I had to go right home and try it. Wow! It's just three ingredients—popcorn, white truffle butter, and salt. It doesn't get any easier than that.

1 package	microwave popcorn, such as Newman's Own Natural
2-ounces	white truffle butter (see note)
1 teaspoon	kosher salt

Prepare the popcorn in your microwave according to the instructions on the package.

Meanwhile, heat the truffle butter in a small pot until *just* melted. When the popcorn is ready, pour it into a large bowl, add the truffle butter and salt, and toss well. Serve warm.

I like Urbani or D'Artagnan white truffle butter. It sounds expensive but it's not.

chipotle & rosemary
roasted nuts

SERVES 8 TO 10

When I have a little extra time before a party, I'll whip up a batch of these really delicious nuts. They're sweet, salty, and spicy—with lots of brown sugar, maple syrup, chipotle powder, and fresh rosemary. Roasting is the process that brings out the most flavor in nuts, and serving them warm is a particularly nice touch.

	Vegetable oil
3 cups	whole roasted unsalted cashews (14 ounces)
2 cups	whole walnut halves (7 ounces)
2 cups	whole pecan halves (7 ounces)
½ cup	whole almonds (3 ounces)
⅓ cup	pure maple syrup
¼ cup	light brown sugar, lightly packed
3 tablespoons	freshly squeezed orange juice
2 teaspoons	ground chipotle powder
4 tablespoons	minced fresh rosemary leaves, divided
	Kosher salt

Chipotle chile powder is different from ordinary chili powder— it's ground dried smoked jalapeños and has a distinctive hot, smoky, sweet flavor.

Preheat the oven to 350 degrees.

Brush a sheet pan generously with vegetable oil. Combine the cashews, walnuts, pecans, almonds, 2 tablespoons of vegetable oil, the maple syrup, brown sugar, orange juice, and chipotle powder on the sheet pan. Toss to coat the nuts evenly. Add 2 tablespoons of the rosemary and 2 teaspoons of salt and toss again.

Spread the nuts in one layer. Roast the nuts for 25 minutes, stirring twice with a large metal spatula, until the nuts are glazed and golden brown. Remove from the oven and sprinkle with 2 more teaspoons of salt and the remaining 2 tablespoons of rosemary. Toss well and set aside at room temperature, stirring occasionally to prevent sticking as they cool. Taste for seasoning. Serve warm or cool completely and store in airtight containers at room temperature.

pink grapefruit margaritas

In the summer I'm always looking for a refreshing cocktail to serve at parties—something traditional but with a nice twist. I played around with pink grapefruit juice and came up with a margarita that hit all the right notes—salty, sweet, and tart. A big bowl of chips and some guacamole wouldn't hurt, either.

1	lime cut in wedges, optional
	Kosher salt, optional
1 cup	ruby red grapefruit juice
½ cup	freshly squeezed lime juice (4 limes)
1 cup	triple sec orange liqueur
3 cups	ice
1 cup	white tequila

If you like a salt rim on the glasses, rub the lime around the edge of each glass and then dip the rim lightly in a plate of kosher salt. Set aside to dry.

Combine the grapefruit juice, lime juice, triple sec, and ice in a blender and purée until smooth. Pour into a large pitcher and stir in the tequila. If you're not serving the margaritas in salted glasses, stir ¼ teaspoon of salt into the pitcher of margaritas. Believe me, it will make a difference.

Serve ice cold.

roasted eggplant caponata

I love Mediterranean dishes because they have lots of flavor and this spicy eggplant dip made with garlic, peppers, olives, pine nuts, and capers is a perfect example. I make it a day or two early so the flavors have time to develop.

To toast pita bread, cut the bread in triangles, brush with olive oil, sprinkle with salt, and bake at 375 degrees for 10 minutes, until lightly browned.

1	large eggplant (1½ pounds)
	Good olive oil
4 ounces	jarred roasted red peppers, chopped
½ cup	large green olives, pitted and chopped
1 cup	chopped yellow onion
⅛ teaspoon	crushed red pepper flakes
1 tablespoon	minced garlic (3 cloves)
3 tablespoons	minced parsley
2 tablespoons	pine nuts, toasted (page 189)
2 tablespoons	freshly squeezed lemon juice
2 tablespoons	drained capers
2 tablespoons	tomato paste
1 tablespoon	red wine vinegar
2 teaspoons	kosher salt
1½ teaspoons	freshly ground black pepper
	Toasted pita triangles (see note), for serving

Preheat the oven to 400 degrees. Line a sheet pan with aluminum foil.

Place the whole eggplant on the pan, prick with a fork in several places, and rub with olive oil. Roast for 45 to 50 minutes, until the eggplant is very soft when pierced with a knife. Set aside to cool. Halve the eggplant, peel, and discard the skin. Place the eggplant, peppers, and olives in the bowl of a food processor fitted with the steel blade and pulse until coarsely chopped. Pour into a mixing bowl.

Meanwhile, heat 1 tablespoon of olive oil in a medium sauté pan. Add the onion and red pepper flakes and cook over medium heat for 5 minutes, until the onion is lightly browned. Add the garlic, cook for 1 minute, and add to the eggplant mixture. Add the parsley, pine nuts, lemon juice, capers, tomato paste, vinegar, salt, and pepper and mix. Cover with plastic wrap and refrigerate for a few hours to allow the flavors to develop. Taste for seasonings and serve at room temperature with toasted pita triangles.

smoked salmon deviled eggs

MAKES 16 APPETIZERS

This is no more complicated to make than that old picnic staple but the addition of smoked salmon and salmon caviar makes it rich and elegant enough for the most sophisticated party. I've also included the perfect way to boil an egg so you don't end up with that dark ring around the yolk.

8	extra-large eggs
½ cup	sour cream
2 ounces	cream cheese, at room temperature
2 tablespoons	good mayonnaise
1 tablespoon	freshly squeezed lemon juice
2 tablespoons	minced fresh chives, plus extra for garnish
4 ounces	good smoked salmon, minced
1 teaspoon	kosher salt
½ teaspoon	freshly ground black pepper
2 ounces	salmon roe

Place the eggs in a pot large enough to hold them in a single layer. Cover the eggs with cold water and bring to a full boil over high heat. As soon as the water boils, turn off the heat, cover the pot, and let the eggs stand for 15 minutes. Drain the eggs and fill the pot with cold water. Set aside until the eggs are cool.

Peel the eggs and then slice them in half lengthwise. Remove the yolks carefully. Place the yolks in the bowl of an electric mixer fitted with the paddle attachment and arrange the whites on a platter in a single layer with the cut sides up and sprinkle with salt.

To the egg yolks, add the sour cream, cream cheese, mayonnaise, lemon juice, chives, salmon, salt, and pepper. Beat on medium speed until fluffy. With a small spoon, fill the egg whites with the egg yolk mixture. Cover loosely with plastic wrap (you don't want to flatten the filling) and refrigerate for 30 minutes for the flavors to blend.

When ready to serve, garnish with a dollop of salmon roe and some extra chopped chives. Sprinkle with salt and pepper and serve.

stilton & walnut crackers

MAKES 24 CRACKERS

I came across this very British cracker in London—a savory shortbread made with Stilton and walnuts. I make extra rolls of dough and freeze them unbaked so I can just defrost, slice, and bake the crackers before guests arrive. Everyone loves these and there are never any leftovers!

¼ pound	(1 stick) unsalted butter, at room temperature
8 ounces	Stilton, crumbled, at room temperature (12 ounces with the rind)
1½ cups	all-purpose flour
2 teaspoons	kosher salt
1 teaspoon	freshly ground black pepper
1	extra-large egg beaten with 1 tablespoon water, for egg wash
½ cup	walnuts, finely chopped

In the bowl of an electric mixer fitted with the paddle attachment, cream the butter and Stilton together for 1 minute, until smooth. With the mixer on low, add the flour, salt, and pepper and continue beating for about 1 minute until the dough is in large crumbles. Add 1 tablespoon of cold water and mix until the dough comes together.

Dump the dough onto a floured board and roll it into a 12-inch-long log. Brush the log completely with the egg wash. Spread the walnuts on a cutting board and roll the log back and forth in the walnuts, pressing lightly, to distribute them evenly on the log. Wrap in plastic and refrigerate for at least 30 minutes or for up to 4 days.

Meanwhile, preheat the oven to 350 degrees and line a sheet pan with parchment paper.

Cut the log into ⅜-inch-thick slices with a small sharp knife and arrange the crackers on the sheet pan. Bake for 22 minutes, until very lightly browned, rotating the pan once during baking. Cool on the pan and serve at room temperature.

When cutting the log into crackers, don't press on the knife; use it like a saw and let the blade do the work.

If you freeze the rolls, defrost them overnight in the refrigerator.

grilled bread with prosciutto

MAKES 6 SLICES

Grilled bread rubbed with garlic is known in Italy as fettunta *and it's the basis for endless easy appetizers. When the bread comes off the grill, I top it with prosciutto, smoked mozzarella, and a drizzle of olive oil, and then put it back on the grill to melt the cheese. How bad could that be?*

6 slices	good Tuscan round bread, sliced ¾ inch thick
1	large garlic clove, cut in half
	Good olive oil
2 ounces	thinly sliced prosciutto, torn in pieces
2 ounces	fresh smoked mozzarella, grated
3 tablespoons	minced fresh parsley

Prepare a charcoal grill with medium-hot coals or turn a gas grill to medium-high heat.

Grill the bread for 2 minutes, until golden on one side. Place the bread grilled side up on a platter and immediately rub the cut side of the garlic clove over the surface of the bread. For really garlicky *fettunta*, rub hard. Drizzle a tablespoon of olive oil over each slice of bread.

Place the torn prosciutto over the grilled side of the bread and top with the grated mozzarella. Return the bread to the hot grill, cover the grill, and cook for 1 to 2 minutes—just long enough to melt the cheese and rewarm the toast. (Be sure the vent is open so the fire doesn't go out!) Drizzle with a little more olive oil, sprinkle with parsley, salt, and pepper, and serve hot.

crostini with tuna tapenade

MAKES 36 APPETIZERS

When I'm grilling, it's fun to have crostini to serve with drinks. This is a classic Mediterranean combination of tuna, olives, and lemon zest. Italian tuna and mascarpone make all the difference.

10 to 12 ounces	canned or jarred Italian tuna packed in olive oil
2 teaspoons	anchovy paste
1 teaspoon	fresh thyme leaves
2 tablespoons	minced fresh parsley, plus extra for garnish
1 tablespoon	grated lemon zest
2 teaspoons	minced garlic (2 cloves)
3 tablespoons	freshly squeezed lemon juice
3 tablespoons	good olive oil, plus extra for brushing bread
⅓ cup	Italian mascarpone cheese
¼ cup	pitted and chopped kalamata olives
1 tablespoon	drained capers
1 teaspoon	kosher salt
1 teaspoon	freshly ground black pepper
36 slices	French bread, cut diagonally

Italian tuna is available in grocery and Italian specialty stores.

Drain all but a tablespoon of olive oil from the tuna and then flake the fish into the bowl of a food processor fitted with the steel blade. Add the anchovy paste, thyme, parsley, lemon zest, and garlic and pulse a few times. Add the lemon juice, 3 tablespoons of olive oil, and the mascarpone and process until almost smooth. Add the olives, capers, salt, and pepper and pulse just to incorporate. Transfer the mixture to a bowl, cover with plastic wrap, and refrigerate for at least 1 hour.

Meanwhile, heat a gas or charcoal grill or preheat the oven to 375 degrees. Brush the bread lightly on one side with olive oil. Grill the crostini on both sides until lightly browned or arrange the bread on a sheet pan and bake for 6 to 8 minutes. Allow to cool slightly.

Mound the tapenade on each toast, sprinkle with parsley, and serve.

savory coeur à la crème

SERVES 8 TO 10

My friends Devon Fredericks and Susan Costner wrote a terrific cookbook called The Loaves and Fishes Cookbook. Coeur à la crème is usually a sweet cream and cream cheese dessert served with a raspberry sauce but they make one that's savory with chutney poured over it to serve with cocktails.

12 ounces	cream cheese, at room temperature
1 cup	heavy cream
	Grated zest of 1 lemon
1 tablespoon	freshly squeezed lemon juice
1 teaspoon	kosher salt
½ teaspoon	freshly ground black pepper
1 (9-ounce) jar	Crosse & Blackwell Major Grey's chutney
	Crackers, for serving

I serve this with Carr's whole wheat crackers.

Place the cream cheese in the bowl of an electric mixer fitted with the whisk attachment. Whip until smooth. With the mixer on low, slowly add the cream and then the lemon zest, lemon juice, salt, and pepper. Whisk until firm.

Line a 6-inch coeur à la crème mold or a 6-inch sieve with a few layers of cheesecloth, allowing the excess to drape over the sides. Pour the cream cheese mixture into the cheesecloth and smooth the top. Fold the excess cheesecloth over the top of the crème. Suspend the sieve over a small bowl, cover with plastic wrap, and refrigerate overnight.

When ready to serve, discard the liquid that has collected in the bowl and invert the crème onto a plate. Pour the chutney over the top, allowing it to drip down the sides. Serve chilled with crackers and a small knife.

starters

mussels & basil bread crumbs, page 80

onion & fennel soup gratin

rich beef barley soup

french mussel bisque

celery & parmesan salad

watermelon & arugula salad

roasted artichoke hearts

buttermilk ranch dressing
with bibb lettuce

soppressata & cheese in puff pastry

herbed ricotta bruschettas

fresh salmon tartare

foie gras with roasted apples

mussels & basil bread crumbs

7

8

Personal recipe file   "Plan B"

planning a menu

When I really want to make entertaining easy, the first thing I decide is whether I need to serve a first course. Oh, I know it makes a meal more elegant and festive, and I do serve them on occasion. But here is my secret: if I have to get a hot dinner on the table—a main course, a vegetable, and a starch—I've never figured out how to do it while I'm sitting calmly at the table sipping my soup. Knowing I have to run back into the kitchen when the timer goes off puts me in a panic! So, this is what I do—for all but the most formal occasions, I simply invite people to the table and serve the main course. If I want three courses, instead of an appetizer I'll serve a salad and a wonderful cheese (which can wait quietly on the side during dinner) after the main course and before dessert. It's special, it's surprising, and it's really easy to serve! Once in a while, if dinner is an entrée that can stay hot in the oven—like Roasted Shrimp with Feta (page 146) or Balsamic Roasted Beef (page 144)—I might make a simple first course like Buttermilk Ranch Dressing with Bibb Lettuce (page 69), but that's all

When I have my heart set on serving one of the first courses in this book, I'll make a totally different plan. I might serve Foie Gras with Roasted Apples (page 78) while we all hang out together in the kitchen drinking a glass of Champagne or Sauternes. Many of the starters in this book can actually be meals in their own right. I love to serve Onion & Fennel Soup Gratin (page 57) as the basis for a cozy winter lunch plus a room-temperature buffet of cheese, ham, and a simple salad on the side. The Herbed Ricotta Bruschettas (page 73) can become a light summer lunch served with a delicious green salad with lemon vinaigrette. And I always have "Plan B"—dinner in the freezer for emergencies!

onion & fennel soup gratin

SERVES 4 TO 6

I love to take a classic recipe and "turn up the volume." Who doesn't love French onion soup gratinée with its topping of onion-soaked bread and gooey melted cheese? I add some fresh fennel to give it more depth of flavor and the results are delicious.

4 tablespoons	(½ stick) unsalted butter
¼ cup	good olive oil
3 pounds	Spanish onions, halved and sliced ¼ inch thick
2 pounds	fennel, tops and cores removed, sliced ¼ inch thick
½ cup	good dry sherry
½ cup	Cognac or brandy
1½ cups	good dry white wine, such as Sauvignon Blanc
8 cups	canned beef broth
3	bay leaves
1 tablespoon	kosher salt
1½ teaspoons	freshly ground black pepper
1	small sourdough or white French boule, crusts removed, sliced ½ inch thick, and toasted
4 to 6 ounces	Gruyère cheese, grated

I use large Spanish onions; they're sweeter and easier to slice than smaller yellow onions.

Heat the butter and oil in a large stockpot over medium-high heat. Add the onions and fennel, and cook over medium heat for 30 to 40 minutes, stirring occasionally, until the onions turn a golden brown. If the onions aren't browning, turn the heat up. Add the sherry and Cognac, scraping up the brown bits in the pan, and simmer uncovered for 5 minutes. Add the white wine and simmer uncovered for 15 more minutes. Add the beef broth, bay leaves, salt, and pepper, bring to a boil, lower the heat, and simmer uncovered for 20 minutes. Remove the bay leaves and taste for seasoning.

Preheat the broiler and position a rack 5 inches below the heat source. Ladle the soup into heat-proof serving bowls, top with the toasted bread, sprinkle generously with grated Gruyère, and broil for 3 to 5 minutes, until the cheese is melted and bubbly. Serve hot.

rich beef barley soup

SERVES 6

When I've made beef barley soup in the past, it never had enough flavor. This soup is made with inexpensive oxtails—which makes it rich and flavorful—plus lots of vegetables like carrots, onions, celery, and fresh thyme. A big pot of this soup on a cold winter night is such a satisfying first course or light supper.

1 tablespoon	good olive oil
2 pounds	beef oxtails
	Kosher salt and freshly ground black pepper
2 cups	chopped leeks, white and light green parts (2 leeks)
2 cups	(½-inch) diced carrots (4 carrots)
1 cup	chopped yellow onion
1 cup	(½-inch) diced celery (2 stalks)
2	garlic cloves, minced
2	sprigs fresh thyme leaves
3	bay leaves
10 cups	canned beef broth
1 cup	pearled barley

I use College Inn beef broth.

Heat the olive oil in a large pot or Dutch oven, such as Le Creuset. Add the oxtails, 1 teaspoon salt, and ½ teaspoon pepper and cook over medium-high heat, stirring occasionally, for 10 minutes until browned all over. Remove the oxtails with a slotted spoon and reserve.

Add the leeks, carrots, onion, celery, and garlic to the fat in the pot and cook over medium heat, stirring occasionally, for 10 minutes, until the vegetables start to brown. Tie the thyme sprigs together with kitchen string and add to the pot along with the bay leaves. Return the oxtails to the pot and add the broth, 1 teaspoon of salt, and 1 teaspoon of pepper. Raise the heat and bring to a boil. Lower the heat, cover, and simmer for 1 hour. Discard the thyme bundle and the bay leaves, and skim off the fat.

Meanwhile, bring 4 cups of water to a boil and add the barley. Simmer uncovered for 30 minutes, drain, and set aside.

When the soup is ready, add the barley and cook the soup for another 15 or 20 minutes, until the barley is tender. Depending on the saltiness of the stock, the soup might need another teaspoon of salt and some pepper. Serve hot, with or without the oxtails.

french mussel bisque

While this isn't the easiest recipe in the book to make, it's really not difficult; with a little scrubbing and chopping, you have a divine soup. The mussels make a delicious broth flavored with white wine, spicy saffron, and lots of vegetables like leeks, carrots, and onions.

1	(750-ml) bottle dry white wine, divided
3 pounds	fresh mussels, cleaned (see note)
6 tablespoons	(¾ stick) unsalted butter
1½ cups	chopped yellow onion (2 onions)
1	large leek, white and light green parts, cleaned and chopped
2	carrots, chopped
4 teaspoons	minced garlic (4 cloves)
½ teaspoon	saffron threads
	Kosher salt and freshly ground black pepper
4	whole canned plum tomatoes, chopped
1½ cups	half-and-half
1 cup	heavy cream
2 tablespoons	minced fresh parsley or dill

To clean mussels, put them in a large bowl of cold water with a handful of flour for 30 minutes. They will drink the water and disgorge any sand.

Bring 1½ cups water and 1 cup of the wine to a boil in a large, shallow pot. Add the mussels, cover the pot, and cook over medium heat for 5 minutes, until the mussels open. When the mussels are cool enough to handle, separate the mussels from the shells and set aside, discarding the shells and any mussels that didn't open. Strain the cooking liquid through a cheesecloth-lined sieve into a bowl and reserve.

Meanwhile, melt the butter in another large heavy-bottomed pot over medium heat. Add the onions, leek, carrots, garlic, saffron, 2 teaspoons salt, and 1 teaspoon pepper and sauté, stirring occasionally, for 5 minutes. Reduce the heat to low, cover, and cook for 20 minutes. Add the tomatoes and cook for another minute.

60 | *how easy is that?*

Add 2 cups of the reserved cooking liquid (discard the rest) and the rest of the wine, bring to a boil, lower the heat, and simmer uncovered for 5 minutes. Add the reserved mussels, the half-and-half, and the cream. Heat until just heated through but not boiling. Stir in the parsley or dill, 1 teaspoon salt, and ½ teaspoon pepper. Serve hot.

celery & parmesan salad

SERVES 4 TO 6

Celery is usually just the crunch in tuna salad or the filler in stuffing, but Italians appreciate it for what it is—a delicious ingredient in its own right. Fresh celery with a tart lemon vinaigrette and salty Parmesan are a great combination of flavors. Slice the celery as thinly as possible with a sharp knife or a mandoline.

½ cup	good olive oil
2 teaspoons	grated lemon zest
¼ cup	plus 1 tablespoon freshly squeezed lemon juice (3 lemons)
2 tablespoons	minced shallots
1 teaspoon	celery seed
½ teaspoon	celery salt
½ teaspoon	anchovy paste
	Kosher salt and freshly ground black pepper
5 cups	thinly sliced celery hearts, tender leaves included, sliced on an angle (about 12 stalks)
4-ounce	chunk aged Parmesan cheese
⅔ cup	toasted walnuts (page 209), coarsely chopped
	Whole flat-leaf parsley leaves

Since this recipe has very few elements, the flavor depends on using the best ingredients. I use aged Italian Parmigiano-Reggiano cheese.

At least 1 hour before you plan to serve the salad, whisk together the olive oil, lemon zest, ¼ cup of lemon juice, the shallots, celery seed, celery salt, anchovy paste, 2 teaspoons salt, and 1 teaspoon pepper. Place the celery in a mixing bowl and toss it with the remaining 1 tablespoon of lemon juice and ½ teaspoon of salt. (Even though these ingredients are in the dressing, believe me— this step makes a difference.) Add enough dressing to moisten well. Cover and refrigerate for at least an hour to allow the celery to crisp and the flavors to develop.

When ready to serve, arrange the celery on a platter, shave the Parmesan onto the celery with a vegetable peeler, then sprinkle with walnuts, parsley leaves, salt, and pepper and serve immediately.

watermelon & arugula salad

It's all the rage in restaurants now to make salads with watermelon and feta.
I have to admit that it leaves me cold—I don't find that watermelon or feta
each make the other taste better. However, when I started playing around with
watermelon, arugula, and freshly squeezed lemon juice, I found that the peppery
greens and the acidic lemon make the sweet watermelon taste more interesting.
This is a refreshing summer salad.

½ pound	baby arugula leaves
2 pounds	seedless watermelon, ¾-inch-diced
	(3 pounds with the rind)
⅓ cup	good olive oil
¼ cup	freshly squeezed lemon juice (2 lemons)
1 teaspoon	kosher salt
½ teaspoon	freshly ground black pepper
½-pound	chunk Parmesan cheese

Place the arugula and watermelon in a large bowl. In a small bowl,
whisk together the olive oil, lemon juice, salt, and pepper. Pour
enough dressing on the arugula to moisten. Toss well and place on
6 salad plates.

With a very sharp knife or a vegetable peeler, shave the Parmesan
into large shards and sprinkle them on the arugula and watermelon.
Sprinkle with salt and serve.

roasted artichoke hearts

Very few frozen vegetables taste as good as fresh ones but one exception is frozen artichoke hearts. Not only do they taste very good but they also save me the annoying job of cutting those prickly artichokes. This is good as a first course for dinner or as part of a big antipasto platter.

2	(9-ounce) boxes frozen artichoke hearts, defrosted
	Good olive oil
	Kosher salt and freshly ground black pepper
1	shallot, minced
3 tablespoons	freshly squeezed lemon juice (2 lemons)
1 tablespoon	good white wine vinegar
1 teaspoon	Dijon mustard
½ cup	chopped fresh basil leaves
3 tablespoons	drained capers
1	jarred roasted red pepper, small-diced
¼ cup	minced red onion
¼ cup	chopped fresh parsley
	Pinch of crushed red pepper flakes

Preheat the oven to 350 degrees.

Place the artichoke hearts on a sheet pan and toss with 1 tablespoon olive oil, ½ teaspoon salt, and ¼ teaspoon black pepper. Roast in a single layer for 20 minutes, turning once with a spatula.

Meanwhile, make the vinaigrette: place the shallot, lemon juice, vinegar, mustard, 1 teaspoon salt, and ½ teaspoon pepper in the bowl of a food processor fitted with the steel blade. Process for 5 seconds. Add the basil and purée. With the processor running, slowly pour in ½ cup olive oil until the dressing is emulsified.

When the artichokes are done, place them in a bowl and toss with enough of the vinaigrette to moisten. Add the capers, red pepper, red onion, parsley, and red pepper flakes and toss. Allow to stand at room temperature for 30 minutes (or refrigerate overnight) for the flavors to develop. Season to taste and serve at room temperature.

buttermilk ranch dressing
with bibb lettuce

MAKES 3 CUPS DRESSING

Instead of making ranch dressing from the package, I much prefer making the real thing—it's easy and has so much flavor from Greek yogurt, buttermilk, scallions, and fresh basil. I serve it simply over good Bibb lettuce but it's also delicious mixed with sliced cabbage for coleslaw. In the summer, I make large batches of this dressing and keep it in the fridge for a quick salad or as a dip for crudités.

3	scallions, white and green parts, chopped
½ cup	chopped fresh basil leaves, lightly packed
2 tablespoons	freshly squeezed lemon juice
1½ tablespoons	Dijon mustard
1 tablespoon	good olive oil
2	garlic cloves, chopped
2½ teaspoons	kosher salt
1 teaspoon	freshly ground black pepper
1 cup	good mayonnaise
½ cup	Greek-style yogurt, such as Fage Total
½ cup	buttermilk, shaken

salad greens for 6

3	small Bibb lettuces, cut in half through the core
2	large ripe tomatoes, thickly sliced
1	red onion, sliced

Place the scallions, basil, lemon juice, mustard, olive oil, garlic, salt, and pepper in the bowl of a food processor fitted with the steel blade. Purée for 15 to 20 seconds to make a smooth mixture. Add the mayonnaise, yogurt, and buttermilk and blend until smooth. Transfer the dressing to a container, cover, and refrigerate for 1 hour for the flavors to develop.

Arrange the lettuce, tomatoes, and onion artfully on salad plates and drizzle with the dressing. Sprinkle with salt and pepper and serve.

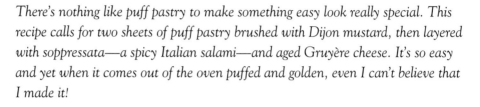

soppressata & cheese
in puff pastry

SERVES 6 FOR FIRST COURSE, 8 FOR COCKTAILS

There's nothing like puff pastry to make something easy look really special. This recipe calls for two sheets of puff pastry brushed with Dijon mustard, then layered with soppressata—a spicy Italian salami—and aged Gruyère cheese. It's so easy and yet when it comes out of the oven puffed and golden, even I can't believe that I made it!

1	package (2 sheets) frozen puff pastry, such as Pepperidge Farm, defrosted
2 tablespoons	Dijon mustard
12	thin (not paper thin) slices soppressata salami (3½ inches in diameter)
6 ounces	Gruyère cheese, grated
1	egg beaten with 1 tablespoon water, for egg wash

If you have time, defrost the puff pastry in the refrigerator overnight.

Preheat the oven to 450 degrees. Place a piece of parchment paper on a sheet pan.

Lay one sheet of puff pastry on a floured board and lightly roll into a 10-inch square. Place it on the sheet pan and brush the pastry with all the mustard, leaving a 1-inch border. Arrange the soppressata in overlapping layers on the mustard and sprinkle the grated cheese evenly on the soppressata, also avoiding the border. Brush the border with the egg wash.

Lightly roll the second piece of puff pastry into a 10-inch square. Lay the pastry directly on top of the first square, lining up the edges. Brush the top with the egg wash, cut three large slits for steam to escape, and chill for 15 minutes.

When the pastry is cold, trim the edges with a very sharp knife to make a clean edge. Bake the pastry in the center of the oven for 20 to 25 minutes, turning once while baking, until puffed and brown. Allow to cool for a few minutes, cut in squares, and serve hot or warm.

herbed ricotta bruschettas

SERVES 6

Who knew it was so easy to make ricotta? I mix it with scallions and fresh herbs like dill and chives—and spread it on toast to serve with a green salad. Home-made ricotta is also good in manicotti for dinner or sweetened with sugar and cocoa powder for a simple Italian dessert.

2 cups	ricotta, store-bought or homemade (recipe follows)
3 tablespoons	minced scallions, white and green parts (2 scallions)
2 tablespoons	minced fresh dill
1 tablespoon	minced fresh chives
	Kosher salt and freshly ground black pepper
1	round sourdough bread
	Good olive oil
1	whole garlic clove, cut in half
	Green Salad Vinaigrette (recipe follows)

Prepare a charcoal grill with hot coals or turn a gas grill to medium-high heat.

Combine the ricotta, scallions, dill, chives, 1 teaspoon salt, and ½ teaspoon pepper and set aside. Cut the bread in half and cut each half into 6 thick slices to make 12 slices total.

When the grill is hot, brush the bread with olive oil and grill on each side for 1½ to 2 minutes, until lightly browned. Remove from the grill and rub each slice of bread with the cut side of the garlic clove. Sprinkle with salt and pepper and spread with the herbed ricotta. Serve 2 warm slices per person with the green salad on the side.

homemade ricotta

MAKES ABOUT 2 CUPS

4 cups	whole milk
2 cups	heavy cream
1 teaspoon	kosher salt
3 tablespoons	good white wine vinegar

Set a large sieve over a deep bowl. Dampen 2 layers of cheesecloth with water and line the sieve with the cheesecloth.

Pour the milk and cream into a stainless-steel or enameled pot such as Le Creuset. Stir in the salt. Bring to a full boil over medium heat, stirring occasionally. Turn off the heat and stir in the vinegar. Allow the mixture to stand for 1 minute until it curdles. It will separate into thick parts (the curds) and milky parts (the whey).

Pour the mixture into the cheesecloth-lined sieve and allow it to drain into the bowl at room temperature for 20 to 25 minutes, occasionally discarding the liquid that collects in the bowl. The longer you let the mixture drain, the thicker the ricotta. (I tend to like mine on the thicker side, but some prefer it moister.) Transfer the ricotta to a bowl, discarding the cheesecloth and any remaining whey. Use immediately or cover with plastic wrap and refrigerate. The ricotta will keep refrigerated for 4 to 5 days.

green salad vinaigrette

SERVES 6

8 to 10 cups	salad greens or mesclun mix
¼ cup	freshly squeezed lemon juice (2 lemons)
½ cup	good olive oil
1 teaspoon	kosher salt
½ teaspoon	freshly ground black pepper

Place the salad greens in a large bowl.

In a small bowl, whisk together the lemon juice, olive oil, salt, and pepper. Pour enough dressing on the salad to moisten. Toss and serve.

fresh salmon tartare

Most salmon tartares are made just with fresh salmon. I combine fresh salmon with smoked salmon for the best of both worlds—the briny flavor of the fresh fish and the earthiness of the smoked salmon. Lots of other ingredients like fresh lime juice, shallots, dill, and mustard make this a really good first course. I make it a few hours in advance to allow the salmon to "cook" and the flavors to blend.

1 pound	skinless fresh salmon fillet
½ pound	smoked salmon, thickly sliced
⅓ cup	freshly squeezed lime juice (3 limes)
⅓ cup	minced shallots (2 shallots)
2 tablespoons	good olive oil
¼ cup	minced fresh dill
3 tablespoons	drained capers
2 tablespoons	Dijon mustard
1 tablespoon	whole-grain mustard
2 teaspoons	kosher salt
1 teaspoon	coarsely ground black pepper
1 loaf	seven-grain bread, thinly sliced and toasted, for serving

Cut the fresh salmon and the smoked salmon in ¼-inch dice. Place the salmon in a mixing bowl and add the lime juice, shallots, olive oil, dill, capers, two mustards, salt, and pepper. Mix well, cover with plastic wrap, and refrigerate for a few hours for the salmon to marinate.

When ready to serve, toast the bread and taste the salmon for seasonings. Serve the tartare with triangles of the toast.

foie gras with roasted apples

SERVES 6

For Jeffrey's and my fortieth wedding anniversary, I invited our best friends over and threw good manners to the wind—the menu was everything we wanted to eat! I served this foie gras with a glass of Sauternes, which also flavors the apple compote. I made the compote in advance and had my friends help cook the foie gras. Foie gras is very expensive but the preparation is so simple that for an occasion like this, it's worth it.

3	large tart red apples, peeled, cored, and each cut into 12 wedges
⅔ cup	sweet dessert wine, such as Sauternes
1½ tablespoons	freshly squeezed lemon juice
1½ tablespoons	honey
14	large pitted prunes (¾ cup)
2	sprigs fresh rosemary
	Freshly ground black pepper
1	whole Grade A duck foie gras (about 1½ pounds), chilled
	Kosher salt

Preheat the oven to 350 degrees.

Stir the apples, wine, lemon juice, and honey together in a bowl. Pour the mixture into one or two baking dishes large enough to hold the apples snugly in a single layer with the apples cut sides down. Scatter the prunes among the apples and tuck the rosemary sprigs into the fruit. Sprinkle with ½ teaspoon of pepper. Cover the baking dishes with aluminum foil and bake for 30 minutes.

Remove the foil from the baking dishes and raise the oven temperature to 375 degrees. Continue baking for 10 to 15 minutes, until the liquid has become syrupy. Set aside. (You can refrigerate the compote for 24 hours and reheat when ready to serve.)

To cook the foie gras, heat a large cast-iron skillet over medium-high heat for 4 minutes. Pull the lobes of foie gras apart and discard the layer of fat inside. Cut each lobe crosswise into ½-inch-thick slices and sprinkle them generously on both sides with salt and pepper. Lower the heat to medium and cook the slices in the hot pan for 45 seconds *only* on each side, until beautifully browned. Place one or two slices of cooked foie gras on each plate with a large spoonful of the warm apple and prune compote. Serve hot.

mussels & basil bread crumbs

SERVES 4

This makes a delicious first course for dinner or a light lunch. My seafood shop sells cleaned, cultivated mussels but it's always a good idea to soak them anyway to make sure all the sand is out of them. You can make the crumb mixture early and then just steam the mussels before serving. I offer a basket of crusty French bread to soak up the juices.

Toast the bread cubes on a sheet pan at 350 degrees for 8 to 10 minutes, tossing once. Allow to cool.

6	slices white bread, crusts removed, cubed, and toasted (see note)
2 tablespoons	chopped garlic (6 cloves)
¼ cup	plus 3 tablespoons good olive oil
2 tablespoons	freshly squeezed lemon juice
9	sun-dried tomato halves in oil, drained and chopped
¾ cup	julienned fresh basil leaves, lightly packed
	Kosher salt and freshly ground black pepper
¼ cup	toasted pine nuts (page 195)
¾ cup	dry white wine, such as Pinot Grigio
3 pounds	mussels, cleaned (page 60)

Combine the toasted bread cubes, garlic, ¼ cup of olive oil, and the lemon juice in a food processor and pulse a few times to make coarse crumbs. Add the sun-dried tomatoes, basil, 1½ teaspoons salt, and ¾ teaspoon pepper and pulse to combine. Add the pine nuts and pulse a few times to combine but not to chop the nuts. Set aside.

Meanwhile, heat 3 tablespoons of olive oil and the wine in a heavy-bottomed pot, such as Le Creuset, and bring to a boil. Add the mussels, cover, and cook over medium-high heat for 4 to 5 minutes, until the mussels have opened. Discard any mussels that don't open. Add the basil bread crumbs and toss gently. Serve hot in shallow bowls with any pan juices.

lunch

middle eastern vegetable salad, page 101

greek panzanella

roasted vegetable frittata

roasted shrimp salad

lobster & shells

baked fontina

tuna & hummus sandwiches

middle eastern vegetable salad

ultimate grilled cheese

mustard chicken salad

snap peas with pancetta

french string bean salad

wild rice salad

tarragon potato salad

9

10

Le Creuset
Dutch ovens

All-Clad sauté pans

good equipment

Some people think that having every kind of pot and pan and kitchen gadget under the sun makes cooking easier, but I'm not one of them. I hate specialized equipment, like pasta machines and garlic presses, that does only one job. I stick to just good-quality essentials and I keep them within easy reach. I love opening my pot drawer and seeing each pot sitting with its own lid on top. I don't have to excavate for the one I want from a pile of mismatched pans that I got for my wedding forty years ago. Even though I have the luxury of a good-size kitchen, the cookware I own is a perfect set of All-Clad pots, sauté pans, and roasting pans, plus one huge stockpot for making soup, which sits right on the stove. They're expensive but after twenty years of use they still look like new—they will literally last me a lifetime. If that kind of investment is an expensive proposition for you right now, check around for a restaurant supply store where you can buy a set of very durable stainless steel pots and utensils for a very reasonable price; if there are a dozen restaurants in your area I'll bet you can find one.

I also look for cookware that does double duty. I love my Le Creuset Dutch ovens; I have a graduated set of four that I use over and over again. They're great for making soups and stews but they're also terrific for serving dinner family-style. One pot, many recipes, lots of uses. Many of us have a KitchenAid mixer, but I keep multiple bowls for mine so when I'm baking I don't have to wash the bowl over and over again. When I've finished baking, I can throw all the bowls in the dishwasher at once and I'm done. (I also have two dishwashers, which is not as expensive as you'd think—it's actually cheaper than building extra cabinets.) For baking, roasting, and all kinds of cooking, I keep a stack of half sheet pans, which you can find in any cookware store. One kind of pan, lots of uses. How easy is that?

greek panzanella

SERVES 6

I love Italian panzanella. What's not to love about toasted bread soaked with vinaigrette and tossed with tomatoes and cucumbers? This Greek version with feta and olives is even better. It's a great first course or a healthy summer lunch.

¾ cup	good olive oil, divided
6 cups	(1-inch) diced rustic bread
	Kosher salt and freshly ground black pepper
1	hothouse cucumber, unpeeled, halved lengthwise, seeded, and sliced ½ inch thick
1	red bell pepper, seeded and large-diced
1	yellow bell pepper, seeded and large-diced
1 pint	cherry or grape tomatoes, halved
½	small red onion, thinly sliced in half-rounds
¼ cup	good red wine vinegar
2 teaspoons	minced garlic (2 cloves)
1 teaspoon	dried oregano, crushed
½ teaspoon	Dijon mustard
½ pound	good feta cheese, ¾-inch-diced
½ cup	kalamata olives, pitted

Heat ¼ cup of the olive oil in a large (12-inch) sauté pan until hot. Add the bread and sprinkle with salt and pepper; cook over low to medium heat, tossing frequently, for 5 to 10 minutes, until nicely browned. Set aside.

Place the cucumber, bell peppers, tomatoes, and red onion in a large bowl and toss together.

For the vinaigrette, place the vinegar, garlic, oregano, mustard, 1 teaspoon salt, and ½ teaspoon pepper in a small bowl and whisk together. Whisking constantly, slowly add the remaining ½ cup of olive oil to make an emulsion.

Add the feta, olives, and bread to the vegetables in the bowl, add the vinaigrette, and toss lightly. Set aside for 30 minutes for the flavors to develop. Season to taste and serve at room temperature.

Be sure to dice rather than crumble the feta.

roasted vegetable frittata

SERVES 6 TO 8

My friend Anna Pump served me my first frittata in 1979 and I've loved them ever since. It's a great one-dish breakfast for a crowd or a delicious lunch with a green salad. This frittata is filled with roasted zucchini, peppers, and red onion and topped with grated Gruyère cheese. It's a terrific meal for vegetarians and the rest of the guests won't mind a bit.

1	small zucchini, 1-inch-diced
1	red bell pepper, seeded and 1½-inch-diced
1	yellow bell pepper, seeded and 1½-inch-diced
1	red onion, 1½-inch-diced
⅓ cup	good olive oil
	Kosher salt and freshly ground black pepper
2 teaspoons	minced garlic (2 cloves)
12	extra-large eggs
1 cup	half-and-half
¼ cup	freshly grated Parmesan cheese
1 tablespoon	unsalted butter
⅓ cup	chopped scallions, white and green parts (3 scallions)
½ cup	grated Gruyère cheese

Preheat the oven to 425 degrees.

Place the zucchini, peppers, and onion on a sheet pan. Drizzle with the olive oil, sprinkle with 1½ teaspoons salt and ½ teaspoon pepper, and toss well. Bake for 15 minutes. Add the garlic, toss again, and bake for another 15 minutes. Remove from the oven and turn the oven to 350 degrees.

Meanwhile, in a large bowl, whisk together the eggs, half-and-half, Parmesan, 1 teaspoon salt, and ½ teaspoon pepper.

In a 10-inch ovenproof sauté pan, melt the butter and sauté the scallions over medium-low heat for 1 minute. Add the roasted vegetables to the pan and toss with the scallions. Pour the egg mixture over the vegetables and cook for 2 minutes over medium-low heat without stirring. Transfer the pan to the oven and bake the frittata for 20 to 30 minutes, until puffed and set in the middle. Sprinkle with the Gruyère and bake for another 3 minutes, until the cheese is just melted. Cut into 6 or 8 wedges and serve hot.

roasted shrimp salad

SERVES 6

While developing recipes for my last cookbook, I found that roasting shrimp instead of boiling them made a shrimp cocktail with so much more flavor—and I didn't have to deal with all that boiling water. I thought, why not try that method for shrimp salad, too? A squeeze of orange juice, some red onion, and vinegary capers added the perfect notes. Buying peeled shrimp is a little more expensive but makes this dish so much easier to make.

2½ pounds	(16 to 20 per pound) peeled shrimp (see note)
1 tablespoon	good olive oil
	Kosher salt and freshly ground black pepper
1 cup	good mayonnaise
1 tablespoon	grated orange zest (2 oranges)
2 tablespoons	freshly squeezed orange juice
1 tablespoon	good white wine vinegar
¼ cup	minced fresh dill
2 tablespoons	drained capers
2 tablespoons	small-diced red onion

Fish stores refer to 16-to-20-count shrimp as "large" and grocery stores call them "extra-large" or "jumbo." To be accurate, order shrimp by the count per pound.

Preheat the oven to 400 degrees.

Pat the shrimp dry with paper towels and place them on a sheet pan. Drizzle with the olive oil, sprinkle with 1 teaspoon salt and ½ teaspoon pepper, and toss together. Spread the shrimp in one layer and roast for 6 to 8 minutes, turning once while cooking, just until pink and firm and cooked through. Allow to cool on the pan for 3 minutes.

Meanwhile, make the sauce. In a large bowl, whisk together the mayonnaise, orange zest, orange juice, vinegar, ½ teaspoon salt, and ½ teaspoon pepper. When the shrimp have cooled, add them to the sauce and toss. Add the dill, capers, and red onion and toss well. The flavors will improve if you cover the salad with plastic wrap and allow it to sit at room temperature for 30 minutes. Otherwise, chill for up to 6 hours and serve at room temperature.

lobster & shells

SERVES 8

In the 1970s, there was a specialty food store in Amagansett, New York, called The Store. No summer party in the Hamptons was complete without Bert Greens's famous Ziti Salad. I made it recently and was disappointed to find that it had less flavor than I remembered—our palates have changed so much! This salad is my homage to Bert, but it has more flavor—from the lobster, corn, tomatoes, and dill—it's very summer in the Hamptons.

	Kosher salt
	Good olive oil
½ pound	small pasta shells, such as Ronzoni
	Kernels from 4 ears of corn (about 3 cups)
6	scallions, white and green parts, thinly sliced
1	yellow or orange bell pepper, seeded and small-diced
1 pint	cherry tomatoes, halved
1 pound	cooked fresh lobster meat, medium-diced
¾ cup	good mayonnaise
½ cup	sour cream
¼ cup	freshly squeezed lemon juice (2 lemons)
	Freshly ground black pepper
¾ cup	minced fresh dill

It's important to use small shells so that the corn kernels can get stuck inside them.

If the sauce is too thick after it's chilled, add a few tablespoons of milk, cream, or lemon juice to thin it.

Bring a large pot of water to a boil and add 1 tablespoon of salt and some olive oil. Add the pasta and cook it for 8 to 10 minutes, until al dente. Add the corn to the pasta and cook it for another 2 minutes, until the corn is tender. Drain the pasta and corn together in a colander and pour them into a large mixing bowl. Add the scallions, diced pepper, tomatoes, and lobster, tossing gently to combine. Allow to cool slightly.

In a small bowl, whisk together the mayonnaise, sour cream, lemon juice, 2 teaspoons salt, and 1 teaspoon pepper until smooth. Pour over the pasta and mix well to bind the ingredients. Stir in the dill, 4 teaspoons salt, and 1 teaspoon pepper. Cover with plastic wrap and chill for up to 6 hours to allow the flavors to develop. Check the seasonings and serve chilled or at room temperature.

baked fontina

Red Cat is a wonderful restaurant in New York City and their cookbook contains many of their iconic recipes like this Baked Fontina. OMG, is this easy—and delicious! For a winter lunch, I serve this with a green salad and some fruit and cookies for dessert. It's like a fondue in a cast-iron pot—you throw everything in and it's ready in six minutes.

1½ pounds	Italian Fontina Val d'Aosta cheese, rind removed and 1-inch-diced
¼ cup	good olive oil
6	garlic cloves, thinly sliced
1 tablespoon	minced fresh thyme leaves
1 teaspoon	minced fresh rosemary leaves
1 teaspoon	kosher salt
1 teaspoon	freshly ground black pepper
1	crusty French baguette

Fontina Val d'Aosta is a soft and very flavorful cheese from Italy. Other fontinas won't have the same depth of flavor.

Preheat the broiler and position the oven rack 5 inches from the heat.

Distribute the cubes of Fontina evenly in a 12-inch cast-iron pan. Drizzle on the olive oil. Combine the garlic, thyme, and rosemary and sprinkle it over the cheese and olive oil. Sprinkle with the salt and pepper and place the pan under the broiler for 6 minutes, until the cheese is melted and bubbling and starts to brown.

Serve the baked Fontina family-style—right out of the oven in the cast-iron pan with crusty chunks of bread for everyone to dip.

tuna & hummus sandwiches

I love Belgium—their style in food and design are the perfect balance of country and elegance. In fact, the design of the barn where I work was inspired by Belgian country farmhouses. I also love the restaurant chain Le Pain Quotidien, which started in Belgium and now fortunately has restaurants all over the world. I had a delicious sandwich there recently and it inspired this recipe. Who would think tuna and hummus would be such a good combination?

14 ounces	jarred or canned Italian tuna in olive oil (page 47)
¼ cup	minced celery
2 tablespoons	minced yellow onion
2 tablespoons	minced cornichons
2 tablespoons	freshly squeezed lemon juice
2 tablespoons	good mayonnaise
1 teaspoon	Dijon mustard
½ teaspoon	kosher salt
¼ teaspoon	freshly ground black pepper
	Sourdough bread, halved and sliced ½ inch thick
	Hummus, store-bought or homemade (recipe follows)
	Fresh radishes, sliced

Drain the oil from the tuna, reserving the oil. Place the tuna in a mixing bowl and flake it with a fork. Add the celery, onion, cornichons, lemon juice, mayonnaise, 2 tablespoons of the reserved oil, the mustard, salt, and pepper and mix well. Cover and refrigerate for a few hours to allow the flavors to develop.

Toast the bread and spread each slice with a layer of hummus. Spread the tuna salad on each piece of bread, garnish with slices of radish, and serve immediately.

hummus

MAKES 2 CUPS

2 cups	canned chickpeas, drained, liquid reserved (15.5-ounce can)
⅓ cup	tahini or sesame paste
4 teaspoons	minced garlic (4 cloves)
6 tablespoons	freshly squeezed lemon juice (3 lemons)
8 dashes	Tabasco sauce
2 teaspoons	kosher salt

Place the chickpeas, 2 tablespoons of the reserved liquid, the tahini, garlic, lemon juice, Tabasco, and salt in the bowl of a food processor fitted with the steel blade and process until coarsely puréed. The hummus should be moist and thick; add more lemon juice or reserved chickpea liquid to thin, if necessary. Cover and refrigerate for several hours for the flavors to blend. Taste for seasonings.

middle eastern vegetable salad

SERVES 4 TO 6

In summer when the tomatoes, scallions, and cucumbers are plentiful at Jim Pike's farmstand in Sagaponack, New York, I love to make fatoush, a Middle Eastern salad with feta and toasted pita bread. The chickpeas make this a very hearty lunch and lots of chopped fresh herbs—parsley, mint, and basil—give it so much flavor. It's up to you whether you serve this in the traditional way with the pita tossed in the salad, or the way I do with the pita on the side.

10	scallions, white and green parts, thinly sliced
1 pound	ripe tomatoes, seeded, cored, and ½-inch-diced
1	hothouse cucumber, halved lengthwise, seeded, and ½-inch-diced
1 can or jar	(12 to 16 ounces) chickpeas, rinsed and drained
⅓ cup	chopped fresh parsley
⅓ cup	chopped fresh mint leaves
⅓ cup	julienned fresh basil leaves
½ cup	freshly squeezed lemon juice (4 lemons)
1 tablespoon	minced garlic (3 cloves)
	Kosher salt and freshly ground black pepper
½ cup	good olive oil
8 ounces	good feta cheese, ½-inch-diced
	Toasted pita bread, for serving (page 38)

Place the scallions, tomatoes, cucumber, chickpeas, parsley, mint, and basil in a large salad bowl and toss to combine.

In a small bowl or measuring cup, whisk together the lemon juice, garlic, 2 teaspoons salt, and 1 teaspoon pepper. Slowly whisk in the olive oil to make an emulsion. Pour the dressing over the salad, tossing gently to coat all the vegetables. Add the feta, sprinkle with salt and pepper, and toss gently. Serve the salad with the toasted pita bread.

I prefer Cirio chickpeas in a jar, if you can find them, but canned chickpeas will be fine.

I use Greek feta. Be sure to dice rather than crumble it.

ultimate grilled cheese

SERVES 6

One day, I invited some friends for lunch and we had a grilled cheese "throw-down." It was so much fun—everybody got to build their favorite sandwich. My friend Barbara Liberman reproduced her mother's grilled cheese with a mustard and mayonnaise sauce, and it won hands down! We used three different cheeses: salty Parmesan, nutty Gruyère, and sharp Cheddar. Grating the cheeses ensures that they melt evenly. If you don't have a panini press, which makes this so easy—no turning!—you can always cook them in a frying pan.

12	slices thick-cut bacon, such as Nodine's applewood smoked
1 cup	good mayonnaise
¼ cup	Dijon mustard
¼ cup	freshly grated Parmesan cheese
1½ teaspoons	kosher salt
½ teaspoon	freshly ground black pepper
1	white pullman loaf or sourdough bread, sliced ½ inch thick (12 slices)
6 tablespoons	salted butter, at room temperature
6 ounces	aged Gruyère or Comté cheese
6 ounces	extra-sharp Cheddar, such as Cabot or Shelburne Farms

Preheat the oven to 400 degrees. Arrange the bacon on a baking rack set over a sheet pan in a single layer and roast for 20 to 30 minutes, until nicely browned. Drain on a plate lined with paper towels and cut in 1-inch pieces.

Meanwhile, combine the mayonnaise, mustard, Parmesan, salt, and pepper in a small bowl. Lay 12 slices of bread on a board and spread each one lightly with butter. Flip the slices and spread each one generously with the mayonnaise mixture. Don't neglect the corners!

Grate the cheeses in a food processor fitted with the largest grating disk and combine. Distribute the bacon evenly on half the slices of bread. Pile ⅓ cup grated cheese evenly on top of the bacon and top with the remaining bread slices, sauce side down.

Meanwhile, heat an electric panini press. When the press is hot, cook the sandwiches for 3 to 5 minutes in batches until the bread is toasted and the cheese is melted. Allow to cool for 2 minutes. Cut in half and serve warm.

mustard chicken salad

SERVES 4 TO 5

This salad was a Barefoot Contessa staple for twenty years. Over the years, I've intensified the flavor by adding more mustard to the sauce and lots of fresh tarragon. A few years ago, I experimented with cooking chicken for salads and I found that the best—and easiest!—way to cook chicken was to roast it on the bone rather than poach skinless chicken breasts. Instead of having big pots of boiling water taking the flavor out of the chicken, roasting them with some olive oil, salt, and pepper actually adds flavor to the chicken.

2	whole (4 split) chicken breasts, bone in, skin on (3 pounds)
	Good olive oil
	Kosher salt and freshly ground black pepper
5 cups	small broccoli florets
1½ cups	good mayonnaise
½ cup	Dijon mustard
¼ cup	whole-grain mustard
2 tablespoons	tarragon vinegar
2 tablespoons	minced fresh tarragon leaves
1 pint	cherry or grape tomatoes, halved

Preheat the oven to 350 degrees.

Place the chicken breasts on a sheet pan and rub the skin with olive oil. Sprinkle liberally with salt and pepper. Roast for 35 to 40 minutes, until the chicken is just cooked. Set aside until cool enough to handle. Discard the skin and bones and dice the chicken in large bite-size pieces.

Meanwhile, fill a large bowl with ice water and bring a large pot of salted water to a boil. Add the broccoli florets to the boiling water and cook for 1 minute only, until crisp-tender. Drain, and place the broccoli into the bowl of ice water until cool. This will stop the cooking and set the bright green color. Drain well.

For the dressing, whisk together the mayonnaise, Dijon mustard, whole-grain mustard, vinegar, 1 tablespoon salt, and 1½ teaspoons pepper. Add enough dressing to the warm chicken to moisten well. (Warm chicken absorbs the sauce best.) Add the tarragon, broccoli, and cherry tomatoes and mix gently to combine. Cover with plastic wrap and refrigerate for a few hours to allow the flavors to develop. Sprinkle with salt and serve at room temperature.

snap peas with pancetta

SERVES 4 TO 5

Union Square Cafe in New York City is one of my all-time favorites. Not only is the food amazing, but the service is, too. When I raved about this snap pea salad, the waiter offered me the recipe. Just when you think their hospitality can't be any more gracious, they do something like that! This is my slight variation on Executive Chef Carmen Quagliata's delicious recipe—it's sliced snap peas with salty pancetta, peppery Pecorino cheese, and a lemony vinaigrette. Everyone who eats it goes crazy!

	Kosher salt
1 pound	sugar snap peas, trimmed
¼ pound	pancetta, sliced
½ cup	good olive oil
2 tablespoons	freshly squeezed lemon juice
2 tablespoons	Champagne or white wine vinegar
¼ cup	minced red onion
5 tablespoons	freshly grated Pecorino Romano cheese
½ teaspoon	freshly ground black pepper

Bring 2 to 3 quarts of water to a boil in a large pot and add 1 tablespoon of salt. Fill a large bowl with ice water and have a sieve or colander ready in the sink. Put the snap peas into the boiling water for only 10 or 15 seconds, drain, and put immediately into the ice water. Cool completely and drain. Cut each snap pea in half lengthwise and place in a large bowl.

Meanwhile, place the pancetta and 1 tablespoon of water in a medium sauté pan and cook over medium heat until the pancetta is browned and crisp, tossing occasionally to brown evenly. The water will evaporate and the pancetta will render some of its fat. Transfer to a plate lined with paper towels to cool.

To make the vinaigrette, whisk together the olive oil, lemon juice, and vinegar. Pour enough vinaigrette on the snap peas to moisten. Add the red onion, crumbled pancetta, Pecorino, 1 teaspoon salt, and the pepper. Toss well, season to taste, and serve.

french string bean salad

SERVES 6

French string beans are those skinny beans sometimes called haricots verts that you can find in the grocery store. They used to be available only in France, which is why they're often known by their French name; they're so much more delicate than their American cousins. A mustard vinaigrette and lots of fresh dill give this salad lots of flavor.

	Kosher salt
1½ pounds	French string beans, both ends trimmed
2 tablespoons	Dijon mustard
2 tablespoons	white wine vinegar
¼ teaspoon	freshly ground black pepper
½ cup	good olive oil
2 tablespoons	minced fresh dill

Fill a large bowl with ice water. Bring a large pot of water to a boil and add 1 tablespoon of salt. Add the beans and cook for 1 minute only. Time it carefully! You want the beans to be crisp-tender. Drain the beans and put them in the ice water until completely cool. Drain the beans again, dry on paper towels, and place them in a large bowl.

In a small bowl, whisk together the mustard, vinegar, ½ teaspoon salt, and the pepper. While whisking, slowly add the olive oil to make an emulsion.

Pour enough dressing over the beans to moisten them well, reserving the rest for another use. Toss with the dill, season to taste, and serve at room temperature. (If the beans aren't served immediately, refrigerate them and add a little extra vinaigrette and a sprinkle of salt before serving.)

wild rice salad

SERVES 4 TO 6

This is an old recipe from the 1970s but it's still delicious. I love the strong nutty flavor of wild rice but it needs to be paired with other ingredients that balance it in a salad. The sweetness of oranges and grapes along with the acidity of a raspberry vinaigrette really do the trick; plus the scallions and pecans give it lots of flavor and texture. This is great on a buffet of summer salads. I also add dried cranberries for a counterpoint of something tart.

1 cup	long-grain wild rice (6 ounces)
	Kosher salt
2	navel oranges
2 tablespoons	good olive oil
2 tablespoons	freshly squeezed orange juice
2 tablespoons	raspberry vinegar
½ cup	seedless green grapes, cut in half
½ cup	pecans, toasted (page 209)
¼ cup	dried cranberries
2 tablespoons	scallions, white and green parts, chopped
½ teaspoon	freshly ground black pepper

Place the wild rice in a medium pot with 4 cups of water and 2 teaspoons of salt and bring to a boil. Simmer uncovered for 50 to 60 minutes, until the rice is very tender. Drain well and place the rice back in the pot. Cover and allow to steam for 10 minutes.

While the rice is still warm, place it in a mixing bowl. Peel the oranges with a sharp knife, removing all the white pith. Cut between the membranes and add the orange sections to the bowl with the rice. Add the olive oil, orange juice, raspberry vinegar, grapes, pecans, cranberries, scallions, ½ teaspoon of salt, and the pepper. Allow to sit for 30 minutes for the flavors to blend. Taste for seasonings and serve at room temperature.

tarragon potato salad

SERVES 6

Most potato salads are downright boring. Fortunately, the difference between a boring one and an absolutely delicious salad is just a few minor tweaks—buttery Yukon Gold potatoes, lots of fresh herbs like tarragon and dill, plus scallions and red onion. Try this recipe once and you'll never make a boring potato salad again.

2 pounds	medium Yukon Gold potatoes (6 to 8 potatoes)
	Kosher salt
1 cup	good mayonnaise
2 tablespoons	freshly squeezed lemon juice
2 tablespoons	tarragon or white wine vinegar
1 teaspoon	freshly ground black pepper
3 tablespoons	chopped scallions, white and green parts
3 tablespoons	minced red onion
2 tablespoons	minced fresh tarragon leaves
2 tablespoons	minced fresh dill

Choose potatoes that are similar in size so they cook evenly.

Place the potatoes in a pot with enough water to cover them. Add 1 tablespoon of salt, bring to a boil, and simmer for 15 to 30 minutes, depending on the size of the potatoes, just until tender when pierced with a small knife or skewer. Drain in a colander. Put a kitchen towel over the colander and allow the potatoes to steam for 10 minutes. When cool enough to handle, peel the potatoes and slice ½ inch thick. Place the potatoes in a mixing bowl.

Meanwhile, combine the mayonnaise, lemon juice, vinegar, 2 teaspoons salt, and the pepper. While the potatoes are still warm, pour the dressing over the potatoes and toss well. Add the scallions, red onion, tarragon, and dill and toss gently. Allow the salad to sit for at least 30 minutes for the flavors to develop. Sprinkle with salt and serve at room temperature.

dinner

steakhouse steaks, page 138

lemon chicken breasts

jeffrey's roast chicken

chicken with shallots

herb-roasted turkey breast

roast turkey with truffle butter

greek lamb with yogurt mint sauce

easy provençal lamb

bangers & mustard mash

steakhouse steaks

sliders

grilled steak & arugula

balsamic roasted beef

roasted shrimp with feta

roasted salmon with green herbs

caesar-roasted swordfish

panko-crusted salmon

weeknight bolognese

spaghetti aglio e olio

spicy turkey meatballs & spaghetti

easy parmesan "risotto"

Post.it notes
for seating

Votive candles

setting the table

The last thing I want to worry about when I'm having friends over is the table setting. How many times have I finished cooking the meal in the nick of time . . . and then realized I *still* had to set the table? We've all seen some pretty over-the-top settings with a million crystal glasses, ceramic dishes filled with candy, lots of flowers, candles, napkin rings, place cards, and chargers. Frankly, I've never known that kind of party to be *more* fun; in fact, it's usually just the opposite—it's intimidating! I'm always afraid I'll reach across the table for the salt and knock over the hostess's precious wine glasses. Tables like those are hard to plan, time-consuming to assemble, and a nightmare to clean up when the party is over.

Instead, when I set a table, I always choose a one-color theme that's appropriate for the season—maybe raspberry in spring or pumpkin in autumn. With my theme in mind, I'll look at what's available in the grocery store in the produce and flower sections while I'm shopping for dinner. Orange roses and clementines in November? I know I can put them together with the white votive candles, white plates, white tablecloth, and white napkins I always have on hand (the napkins have an orange detail on them so they'll be perfect). A garden party in the summer? With my green striped cloth, all I'll need from the store are big bunches of basil, dill, parsley, and chives to arrange in drinking glasses down the middle of the table. It's not fussy, it's easy to assemble, and no one feels like the setting is more precious than the company—which, frankly, is the point.

And here's my trick: I always have Post-it notes in the kitchen drawer to make a seating arrangement; one color for girls, one for boys. I put a name on each note and then I can move them around easily until I find the perfect seating arrangement for a great party.

lemon chicken breasts

SERVES 4

When I need to get dinner together in a hurry, this is about as easy as it gets. White wine, garlic, and oregano give this chicken great flavor. I make some basmati rice or Couscous with Toasted Pine Nuts (page 195) to soak up all those delicious lemony juices plus a vegetable like steamed haricots verts and I'm done.

¼ cup	good olive oil
3 tablespoons	minced garlic (9 cloves)
⅓ cup	dry white wine
1 tablespoon	grated lemon zest (2 lemons)
2 tablespoons	freshly squeezed lemon juice
1½ teaspoons	dried oregano
1 teaspoon	minced fresh thyme leaves
	Kosher salt and freshly ground black pepper
4	boneless chicken breasts, skin on (6 to 8 ounces each)
1	lemon

Preheat the oven to 400 degrees.

Warm the olive oil in a small saucepan over medium-low heat, add the garlic, and cook for just 1 minute but don't allow the garlic to turn brown. Off the heat, add the white wine, lemon zest, lemon juice, oregano, thyme, and 1 teaspoon salt and pour into a 9 × 12-inch baking dish.

Pat the chicken breasts dry and place them skin side up *over* the sauce. Brush the chicken breasts with olive oil and sprinkle them liberally with salt and pepper. Cut the lemon in 8 wedges and tuck it among the pieces of chicken.

Bake for 30 to 40 minutes, depending on the size of the chicken breasts, until the chicken is done and the skin is lightly browned. If the chicken isn't browned enough, put it under the broiler for 2 minutes. Cover the pan tightly with aluminum foil and allow to rest for 10 minutes. Sprinkle with salt and serve hot with the pan juices.

jeffrey's roast chicken

SERVES 3

Recently, I met some beautiful young women from Glamour magazine. They make a roast chicken they call "Engagement Chicken" because every time one of them makes it for her boyfriend, she gets engaged! How wonderful is that? That's the best reason I ever heard to roast a chicken! This recipe is very much like my original Perfect Roast Chicken (The Barefoot Contessa Cookbook)— with a few tweaks to make it even more delicious.

1	(4- to 5-pound) roasting chicken
	Kosher salt and freshly ground black pepper
2	lemons
1	whole head of garlic, cut in half crosswise
	Good olive oil
2	Spanish onions, peeled and thickly sliced
½ cup	dry white wine
½ cup	chicken stock, preferably homemade (page 181)
1 tablespoon	all-purpose flour

Preheat the oven to 425 degrees.

Remove and discard the chicken giblets. Pat the outside dry. Liberally salt and pepper the inside of the chicken. Cut the lemons in quarters and place 2 quarters in the cavity along with the garlic. Brush the chicken with olive oil and sprinkle liberally with salt and pepper. Tie the legs together with kitchen string and tuck the wing tips under the body of the chicken. Place the chicken in a small (11 × 14-inch) roasting pan. (If the pan is too large, the onions will burn.) Place the reserved lemons and the sliced onions in a large bowl and toss with 2 tablespoons of olive oil, 1 teaspoon of salt, and ½ teaspoon of pepper. Pour the mixture around the chicken.

Roast the chicken for about 1 hour and 15 minutes, until the juices run clear when you cut between a leg and a thigh. Remove the chicken to a platter, leaving the lemons and onions in the pan. Cover the chicken with aluminum foil, and allow to rest for 10 minutes while you prepare the sauce.

Place the pan on top of the stove over medium-high heat. Add the wine and stir with a wooden spoon to scrape up the brown bits. Add the stock and sprinkle on the flour, stirring constantly for a minute, until the sauce thickens. Add any juices that collect on the platter under the chicken and taste for seasoning. Carve the chicken onto the platter and spoon the onions and sauce over it. If the lemons are tender enough to eat, serve them, too. Sprinkle with salt and serve hot or warm.

chicken with shallots

This chicken is good enough for the fanciest company but easy enough to make for a quick dinner. I love the rich cream sauce flavored with white wine, shallots, and lemon and spooned over simple roast chicken breasts. Ask the butcher to bone the chicken breasts, leaving the skin on, and you're good to go.

4	boneless chicken breasts, skin on (6 to 8 ounces each)
	Kosher salt and freshly ground black pepper
3 tablespoons	vegetable or canola oil
½ cup	dry white wine
⅓ cup	freshly squeezed lemon juice (3 lemons)
¼ cup	minced shallots (1 large)
3 tablespoons	heavy cream
4 tablespoons	(½ stick) unsalted butter, diced, at room temperature

Chicken breasts available commercially vary wildly in size, which makes it difficult to know how long to cook them. I find Bell & Evans chickens delicious and the chicken breasts are all the same size— not too big or too small.

Preheat the oven to 425 degrees.

Pat the chicken breasts dry with paper towels and sprinkle them generously on both sides with salt and pepper. In a 12-inch cast-iron skillet, heat the oil over medium-high heat for 2 minutes, until it begins to smoke. Place the chicken breasts, skin side down, in the skillet and cook for 4 to 5 minutes without moving, until golden brown.

Using tongs, turn the chicken breasts skin side up, place the skillet in the oven, and roast for 12 to 15 minutes, until the chicken is cooked through.

Meanwhile, in a medium sauté pan, combine the white wine, lemon juice, and shallots and cook over medium-high heat for about 5 minutes, until only 2 tablespoons of liquid remain in the pan. If it reduces too much, add an extra splash of white wine or water. Add the cream, 1 teaspoon salt, and ¼ teaspoon pepper and bring to a full boil. Remove from the heat, add the diced butter, and swirl the pan until the butter is incorporated. Don't reheat or the sauce will "break"! Sprinkle with salt and serve the chicken hot with the sauce spooned over it.

herb-roasted turkey breast

Why do we only serve turkey on Thanksgiving? A whole turkey breast roasted with fresh rosemary, sage, and thyme is a great weeknight dinner and the leftovers make delicious sandwiches the next day. Roasting the turkey at 325 degrees and allowing it to rest for fifteen minutes ensures that it will be very moist.

1	whole bone-in turkey breast (6½ to 7 pounds)
2 tablespoons	good olive oil
1 tablespoon	minced garlic (3 cloves)
2 teaspoons	freshly squeezed lemon juice
2 teaspoons	dry mustard
1 tablespoon	chopped fresh rosemary leaves
1 tablespoon	chopped fresh sage leaves
1 teaspoon	chopped fresh thyme leaves
1½ teaspoons	kosher salt
½ teaspoon	freshly ground black pepper
¾ cup	dry white wine

Preheat the oven to 325 degrees. Place the turkey breast on a rack in a roasting pan, skin side up.

In a small bowl, combine the olive oil, garlic, lemon juice, mustard, rosemary, sage, thyme, salt, and pepper. Rub the mixture evenly all over the skin of the turkey breast. (You can also loosen the skin and smear half of the paste underneath, directly on the meat.) Pour the wine into the bottom of the roasting pan.

Roast the turkey for 1½ to 1¾ hours, until the skin is golden brown and an instant-read meat thermometer registers 165 degrees when inserted into the thickest and meatiest area of the breast. Check the breast after an hour or so; if the skin is overbrowning, cover it loosely with aluminum foil.

When the turkey is done, remove from the oven, cover the pan with aluminum foil, and allow the turkey to rest at room temperature for 15 minutes. Slice and serve warm with the pan juices.

roast turkey with truffle butter

SERVES 8

My friend Sarah Chase worked with the Butterball hotline for years. For Thanksgiving they test various methods to figure out the best way to cook turkeys and every year the same method wins: 325 degrees and no basting! Lots of truffle butter under the skin also makes this the moistest turkey you'll ever eat. The best news is that the pan juices are so delicious with fragrant truffles that you don't even need to make gravy.

1	(12- to 14-pound) fresh kosher turkey (see note), giblets removed
3 ounces	white truffle butter, at room temperature
	Kosher salt and freshly ground black pepper
1	large yellow onion, unpeeled and cut into 8 wedges
1	whole head of garlic, unpeeled and cut in half crosswise
	Large bunch of fresh thyme
	Good olive oil

Instead of brining a turkey, I use a kosher one such as Empire—it's already been salted!

Preheat the oven to 325 degrees. Drain any juices from the turkey cavity and place the turkey on a rack in a large, shallow roasting pan, breast side up. Pat dry with paper towels.

Working from the large cavity end, gently run your fingers between the skin and the meat to loosen the skin, taking care not to tear it. (Don't do this with rings on your fingers!) Place the softened truffle butter under the skin and gently massage the skin to spread the butter evenly over the whole breast.

Sprinkle the cavity generously with salt and pepper. Place the onion, garlic, and half of the thyme sprigs in the cavity. Tie the legs together with kitchen string and tie one length of string around the bird and the wings to keep the wings close to the body.

Brush the turkey all over with olive oil and sprinkle with 2 teaspoons of salt and 1 teaspoon of pepper. Remove 1 tablespoon of leaves from the remaining thyme sprigs, chop them, and sprinkle on the turkey. Roast the turkey for 2½ to 3 hours, until a meat thermometer placed in the center of the breast registers 160 degrees. Don't baste the turkey at all! About halfway through, when the breast is golden brown, cover the breast loosely with aluminum foil to prevent the skin from burning.

Remove the turkey from the oven, cover tightly with aluminum foil, and allow to rest in the pan for 15 to 20 minutes. Carve and serve with the pan juices.

greek lamb
with yogurt mint sauce

SERVES 4 TO 6

This is a great dish for entertaining; you marinate the lamb and make the sauce a day in advance. All you need to do before dinner is grill the lamb and serve it hot with the cold yogurt sauce. The lamb is flavored with lots of garlic, rosemary, and lemon, and it's very delicious and summery. Choose a dry red wine that you'll drink with dinner.

4	large garlic cloves
3 tablespoons	chopped fresh rosemary leaves
1½ teaspoons	dried oregano
	Kosher salt and freshly ground black pepper
½ cup	freshly squeezed lemon juice (4 lemons)
½ cup	good olive oil
½ cup	dry red wine
2	racks of lamb, frenched and cut into 8 chops each
	Yogurt Mint Sauce (recipe follows)

Place the garlic, rosemary, oregano, 1½ teaspoons salt, and ¾ teaspoon pepper in the bowl of a food processor fitted with the steel blade and pulse until the herbs are finely minced. Add the lemon juice, olive oil, and red wine and combine. Place the chops in a glass or ceramic dish just large enough to hold them in a single layer. Pour the marinade over the chops, turning to coat both sides. Cover with plastic wrap and refrigerate for at least 2 hours but preferably overnight.

You can also broil the lamb 6 inches from the heat for 10 minutes.

When ready to cook, prepare a grill with one layer of hot coals or turn a gas grill to medium-high heat. Remove the lamb from the marinade, sprinkle generously with salt and pepper, and grill for 4 to 5 minutes on each side. Remove to a platter, cover tightly with aluminum foil, and set aside to rest for 10 minutes. Serve hot with the cold Yogurt Mint Sauce.

yogurt mint sauce

MAKES 1 CUP

6	scallions, white and green parts, chopped
½ cup	chopped fresh mint leaves
2 tablespoons	minced fresh dill
	Pinch of crushed red pepper flakes
1 tablespoon	good olive oil
1 tablespoon	freshly squeezed lemon juice
7 ounces	Greek-style yogurt, such as Fage Total
1 teaspoon	kosher salt
½ teaspoon	freshly ground black pepper

Place the scallions, mint, dill, red pepper flakes, olive oil, and lemon juice in the bowl of a food processor fitted with the steel blade and purée until it's a coarse paste. Add the yogurt, salt, and pepper and pulse until combined. Transfer to a bowl, cover, and refrigerate for a few hours to allow the flavors to develop.

easy provençal lamb

SERVES 8

My friend Myriam Richard-Delorme in Paris is a great cook and she gave me this recipe. All you do is put a leg of lamb in a roasting pan with lots of cut-up tomatoes, onions, garlic, rosemary—and then pour honey over it to caramelize the lamb and tomatoes while they roast. Everything cooks in one pan and a few hours later you have the most succulent roast lamb, plus the tomatoes and pan juices become the sauce. OMG is it fabulous!

You'll want to use a liquid—rather than a solid—honey for this recipe so it can be drizzled on the lamb.

1	(6- to 7-pound) bone-in leg of lamb, trimmed and tied
½ cup	Dijon mustard
3 tablespoons	chopped garlic (9 cloves), divided
1 tablespoon	chopped fresh rosemary leaves
1 tablespoon	balsamic vinegar
	Kosher salt and freshly ground black pepper
3 pounds	ripe red tomatoes, cored and 1-inch-diced
½ cup	good olive oil
½ cup	good honey (see note), divided
1	large Spanish onion, sliced
4	sprigs fresh thyme
2	sprigs fresh rosemary

Preheat the oven to 450 degrees.

Place the leg of lamb in a large roasting pan fat side up and pat it dry with paper towels. Combine the mustard, 1 tablespoon of the garlic, the rosemary, balsamic vinegar, 1 tablespoon salt, and ½ teaspoon pepper in a mini food processor and pulse until the garlic and rosemary are minced. Spread the mixture on the lamb.

Place the tomatoes, olive oil, ¼ cup of the honey, the onion, the remaining 2 tablespoons garlic, 2 tablespoons salt, and 2 teaspoons pepper in a bowl and toss well. Pour the tomato mixture around the lamb and tuck in the thyme and rosemary sprigs. Drizzle the lamb with the remaining ¼ cup of honey.

Roast for 20 minutes. Turn the heat down to 350 degrees and roast for another 1 to 1¼ hours, until a meat thermometer registers 130 to 135 degrees for medium-rare. Place the lamb on a cutting board, cover with aluminum foil, and allow to rest for 15 minutes. Discard the herb stems and return the tomatoes to the oven to keep warm. Slice the lamb, arrange on a platter, sprinkle with salt and pepper, and serve with the tomatoes and pan juices spooned on top.

bangers & mustard mash

SERVES 4 TO 6

My television producer, Olivia Grove, met her husband, Matt Ball, while they were working on my television show. I went to their wedding in London and for the dinner they served "bangers & mash," which is English sausages and mashed potatoes. It was the best wedding food I'd ever eaten and it had so much style. Of course, they were delicious lamb and veal sausages and sublime mashed potatoes, but I loved the earthiness of the dish for such an elegant event. This is my humble version of that wonderful meal.

2 pounds	Yukon Gold potatoes, peeled and quartered
	Kosher salt
4 tablespoons	(½ stick) unsalted butter, diced
½ cup	whole milk
4 ounces	crème fraîche
2 teaspoons	Dijon mustard
2 teaspoons	whole-grain mustard
1 teaspoon	dry mustard
1 teaspoon	freshly ground black pepper
2 pounds	fresh veal or chicken sausages (8 large sausages)

You can also grill a few thick slices of red onion with the sausages and serve them together with the mashed potatoes.

Place the potatoes in a large saucepan with 1 tablespoon of salt and enough water to cover the potatoes. Bring to a boil and simmer for 20 to 25 minutes, until the potatoes are very tender. Drain the potatoes in a colander and return them to the saucepan. Add the butter, milk, and crème fraîche and beat the potatoes in the pan with a handheld mixer until very smooth and creamy. Add a little extra milk if they're too stiff. Mix in the Dijon mustard, whole-grain mustard, dry mustard, 1 tablespoon salt, and the pepper. Place the potatoes in a heat-proof bowl set over simmering water and keep hot for up to 30 minutes, until ready to serve. (You may need to add more hot milk from time to time.)

Meanwhile, prepare a grill with hot coals or heat a gas grill to medium-high and cook the sausages for about 5 minutes on each side, until browned and cooked through. Transfer to a plate, wrap with aluminum foil, and allow to rest for 5 minutes.

To serve, mound a generous portion of potatoes on a dinner plate and top with grilled sausages that have been cut in half diagonally.

steakhouse steaks

SERVES 4

What is it that makes the steak you get at a good steakhouse so delicious? Of course, it's usually very good-quality meat that's been aged well, but it's also that crusty exterior that's perfectly seasoned and not burnt, with a tender, juicy interior that tastes of nothing but great steak. The secret? They're pan-roasted, not grilled. My friends say these are the best steaks they ever ate.

4	(2-inch-thick) filets mignons, tied (10 ounces each)
2 tablespoons	vegetable oil
2 tablespoons	fine fleur de sel
2 tablespoons	coarsely cracked black peppercorns
4 tablespoons	(½ stick) unsalted butter, at room temperature
	Roquefort Chive Sauce (recipe follows)

It's important that your meat thermometer is accurate. Test it by putting it in a pot of rapidly boiling water; it should register 212 degrees exactly.

Preheat the oven to 400 degrees.

Heat a large cast-iron skillet over high heat for 5 to 7 minutes.

Meanwhile, pat dry the filets mignons with paper towels. Brush the filets lightly all over with the oil. Combine the fleur de sel and cracked pepper on a plate and roll the filets on all sides in the mixture, pressing lightly to help the salt and pepper adhere. The steaks should be evenly coated with the salt and pepper.

When the pan is extremely hot, add the steaks and sear evenly on all sides (top, bottom, and sides) for about 2 minutes per side. (Be sure the cooking area is well ventilated.) You'll probably need about 3 turns to sear the sides and about 10 minutes total.

Remove the pan from the heat and arrange all the filets flat in the pan. Top each with a tablespoon of butter, then place the pan in the oven. Cook the filets for 8 to 12 minutes to 120 degrees for rare and 125 degrees for medium-rare. Remove the steaks to a platter, cover tightly with aluminum foil, and allow to rest for 5 to 10 minutes. Remove the string and serve plain or topped with Roquefort Chive Sauce.

roquefort chive sauce

MAKES ¾ CUP

1½ cups	heavy cream
2 ounces	Roquefort cheese, crumbled (4 ounces with rind)
½ teaspoon	kosher salt
½ teaspoon	freshly ground black pepper
1 tablespoon	chopped fresh chives

Pour the cream into a small heavy-bottomed saucepan and bring to a boil over medium-high heat. Simmer for about 20 minutes, stirring occasionally, until the cream is reduced by half and is thickened.

Off the heat, add the Roquefort and stir until melted. Add the salt and pepper and taste for seasonings. Stir in the chives. Spoon the warm sauce over the steaks.

sliders

SERVES 4 TO 6

Sliders are small burgers and they're not only delicious but also fun to eat! It's important to get the right seasonings like mustard, thyme, and garlic to bring out the "steak" quality of good grass-fed beef. Because they're small, they cook quickly and stay really juicy.

2 pounds	ground Niman Ranch beef or other premium beef (80% lean and 20% fat)
3 tablespoons	good olive oil
1 tablespoon	Dijon mustard
1 tablespoon	minced garlic (3 cloves)
1 teaspoon	chopped fresh thyme leaves
	Kosher salt and freshly ground black pepper
6 ounces	grated Gruyère cheese
12	mini brioche, onion, or hamburger buns, split
3	small red tomatoes, sliced
4 ounces	baby arugula
	Good ketchup, for serving (see note)

I love Stonewall Kitchen's Country Ketchup.

Prepare a grill with hot coals or turn a gas grill to medium-high heat.

Place the ground beef in a bowl, add the olive oil, mustard, garlic, thyme, 1 teaspoon salt, and ½ teaspoon pepper, and mix gently with a fork, taking care not to compress the ingredients. Divide the mixture into quarters and shape each quarter into 3 patties.

When the grill is hot, place the burgers on the grill and cook for 4 to 6 minutes on each side. Top each burger with some grated Gruyère for the last 2 minutes and close the lid to melt the cheese. Transfer the burgers to a platter, cover tightly with aluminum foil, and allow to rest for 5 minutes.

Toast the buns cut side down on the grill for 15 seconds. Place each burger on top of a bun and top with a slice of tomato and some arugula. Sprinkle with salt and pepper and cover with the top bun. Serve hot with ketchup on the side.

grilled steak & arugula

SERVES 4

A hot grilled steak with a cold arugula salad underneath is the quintessential one-dish summer dinner—sort of an updated version of my Parmesan Chicken in Barefoot Contessa Family Style. *This is one of my favorite meals—Jeffrey loves the juicy steak together with the peppery baby arugula, fresh lemon, and Parmesan cheese.*

2	(1-inch-thick) boneless rib-eye steaks
½ cup	good olive oil, plus extra for brushing the steaks
	Kosher salt and freshly ground black pepper
¼ cup	freshly squeezed lemon juice (2 lemons)
½ teaspoon	Dijon mustard
8 ounces	baby arugula
1	(4-ounce) chunk good Parmesan cheese

Prepare a charcoal grill with hot coals or turn a gas grill to medium-high heat.

Brush the steaks lightly with olive oil and sprinkle both sides liberally with salt and pepper. Set aside at room temperature for 15 minutes.

Meanwhile, whisk together the ½ cup of olive oil, the lemon juice, mustard, 1 teaspoon salt, and ½ teaspoon pepper. Set aside.

When the grill is hot, place the steaks on the grill. Cook for 5 minutes on each side and then close the lid, making sure the vents are open slightly. Cook for 5 to 15 minutes more for medium-rare, depending on the heat of the coals, until the centers of the steaks register 125 degrees on an instant-read thermometer. Remove to a plate, cover tightly with foil, and allow to rest for 10 minutes before slicing thickly.

Toss the arugula in a large bowl with enough of the dressing to moisten; divide among 4 plates. Place half a steak on top of each salad. Shave the Parmesan onto each steak with a vegetable peeler, sprinkle with salt, and serve hot.

balsamic roasted beef

SERVES 5 TO 6

My friend Brent Newsom is the best caterer in the Hamptons—which is saying something! He makes a dish like this roasted filet of beef covered with mustard, balsamic vinegar, and cracked pepper for his very happy clients. Be sure your oven is very clean before turning it to 500 degrees or the fire department will show up!

2½ pounds	filet of beef, trimmed and tied
2 tablespoons	Dijon mustard
1 tablespoon	aged balsamic vinegar
1 teaspoon	kosher salt
1 tablespoon	coarsely cracked black pepper

Preheat the oven to 500 degrees. Line a sheet pan with aluminum foil.

Place the beef on the sheet pan. Combine the mustard, vinegar, and salt in a small bowl. Spread the mixture on the filet and brush it evenly over the top and sides. Sprinkle the cracked pepper evenly all over the meat.

Roast the filet for 30 minutes exactly for medium-rare (25 minutes for rare and 35 minutes for medium). Remove the pan from the oven, cover tightly with aluminum foil, and allow the beef to rest on the pan for 10 minutes. Slice and serve hot or warm.

roasted shrimp with feta

SERVES 4

Assemble this early in the day and throw it in the oven before dinner. I serve big chunks of crusty bread so everyone can mop up all that delicious sauce. I love the Greek combination of tomatoes, garlic, oregano, wine, and feta; they enhance— but don't overpower—the briny flavor of the shrimp. Using peeled shrimp makes this dish so easy.

For 1 cup of fresh bread crumbs, remove the crusts from 4 slices of white bread and process them in a food processor fitted with the steel blade until the bread is in crumbs.

4 tablespoons	good olive oil, divided
1½ cups	medium-diced fennel
1 tablespoon	minced garlic (3 cloves)
¼ cup	dry white wine
1	(14½-ounce) can diced tomatoes
2 teaspoons	tomato paste
1 teaspoon	dried oregano
1 tablespoon	Pernod
1 teaspoon	kosher salt
½ teaspoon	freshly ground black pepper
1¼ pounds	(16 to 20 per pound) peeled shrimp with tails on
5 ounces	good feta cheese, coarsely crumbled
1 cup	fresh bread crumbs (see note)
3 tablespoons	minced fresh parsley
1 teaspoon	grated lemon zest
2	lemons

Preheat the oven to 400 degrees.

Heat 2 tablespoons of the olive oil in a 10- or 12-inch heavy oven-proof skillet over medium-low heat. Add the fennel and sauté for 8 to 10 minutes, until the fennel is tender. Add the garlic and cook for 1 minute. Add the wine and bring to a boil, scraping up any browned bits. Cook for 2 to 3 minutes, until the liquid is reduced by half. Add the tomatoes with the liquid, tomato paste, oregano, Pernod, salt, and pepper to the skillet. Simmer over medium-low heat, stirring occasionally, for 10 to 15 minutes.

Arrange the shrimp, tails up, in one layer over the tomato mixture in the skillet. Scatter the feta evenly over the shrimp. In a small bowl, combine the bread crumbs, parsley, and lemon zest with the remaining 2 tablespoons of olive oil and sprinkle over the shrimp.

Bake for 15 minutes, until the shrimp are cooked and the bread crumbs are golden brown. Squeeze the juice of 1 lemon over the shrimp. Serve hot with the remaining lemon cut into wedges.

roasted salmon with green herbs

SERVES 6

This is a great last-minute dinner. I can pick up the salmon on the way home, and I've usually got some herbs in the garden, and the rest of the ingredients in the pantry. Roasting is so much less stressful than grilling and the salmon stays very moist. I have needlenose-pliers in a drawer for removing any pesky pinbones that the fish store misses.

1	(2- to 2½-pound) skinless salmon fillet
	Kosher salt and freshly ground black pepper
¼ cup	good olive oil
2 tablespoons	freshly squeezed lemon juice
½ cup	minced scallions, white and green parts (4 scallions)
½ cup	minced fresh dill
½ cup	minced fresh parsley
¼ cup	dry white wine
	Lemon wedges, for serving

Preheat the oven to 425 degrees.

Place the salmon fillet in a glass, ceramic, or stainless-steel roasting dish and season it generously with salt and pepper. Whisk together the olive oil and lemon juice and drizzle the mixture evenly over the salmon. Let it stand at room temperature for 15 minutes.

In a small bowl, stir together the scallions, dill, and parsley. Scatter the herb mixture over the salmon fillet, turning it so that both sides are generously coated with the green herbs. Pour the wine around the fish fillet.

Roast the salmon for 10 to 12 minutes, until almost cooked in the center at the thickest part. The center will be firm with just a line of uncooked salmon in the very center. (I peek by inserting the tip of a small knife.) Cover the dish tightly with aluminum foil and allow to rest for 10 minutes. Cut the salmon crosswise into serving pieces and serve hot with lemon wedges.

caesar-roasted swordfish

SERVES 6

I love swordfish because it's flavorful enough to stand up to a good sauce and doesn't dry out when it's cooked. I make the Caesar sauce in the food processor with lots of garlic and anchovies, then just slather it on the swordfish and bake it.

2	large garlic cloves, chopped
¼ cup	chopped fresh parsley
1 tablespoon	anchovy paste
2 teaspoons	Dijon mustard
1 cup	good mayonnaise
1 tablespoon	grated lemon zest (2 lemons)
3 tablespoons	freshly squeezed lemon juice
	Kosher salt and freshly ground black pepper
3 pounds	center-cut swordfish steaks, ¾ to 1 inch thick, cut into 6 portions
½ cup	chopped scallions, white and green parts (4 scallions)
2 tablespoons	good olive oil
3 tablespoons	drained capers
	Lemon wedges, for serving

The frizzled capers add a great flavor and texture to the dish.

Preheat the oven to 500 degrees. (Be sure your oven is very clean.) Line a sheet pan with aluminum foil.

For the Caesar sauce, place the garlic, parsley, anchovy paste, and mustard in the bowl of a food processor fitted with the steel blade and pulse until the garlic is minced. Add the mayonnaise, lemon zest, lemon juice, 1 teaspoon salt, and ½ teaspoon pepper and pulse to make a smooth sauce.

Place the swordfish steaks on the pan and sprinkle both sides generously with salt and pepper. Set aside one third of the sauce to serve with the cooked fish. Spread the fish on one side with half the remaining sauce, turn the fish, and spread the remaining sauce on the second side. Sprinkle with the scallions and allow to stand for 10 minutes.

Roast the fish for 10 to 12 minutes, until the center is just barely cooked. Cover the fish with aluminum foil and allow to rest on the pan for 10 minutes.

Meanwhile, heat the oil in a small sauté pan until very hot, add the capers, and cook for 30 to 60 seconds, until they start to pop and are a little crisp. Serve the swordfish hot with the lemon wedges, frizzled capers, and the reserved Caesar sauce.

panko-crusted salmon

SERVES 4

I've recently become a fan of panko, Japanese dried bread flakes. They're available in the Asian section of your grocery store and probably also at your local seafood shop. They save me the hassle of making bread crumbs and toasting them. Panko, parsley, and lemon zest make the perfect crunchy topping for roasted salmon.

⅔ cup	panko (Japanese dried bread flakes)
2 tablespoons	minced fresh parsley
1 teaspoon	grated lemon zest
	Kosher salt and freshly ground black pepper
2 tablespoons	good olive oil
4	(6- to 8-ounce) salmon fillets, skin on
2 tablespoons	Dijon mustard
2 tablespoons	vegetable oil
	Lemon wedges, for serving

Preheat the oven to 425 degrees.

In a small bowl, mix together the panko, parsley, lemon zest, ½ teaspoon salt, and ½ teaspoon pepper. Drizzle with the olive oil and stir until the crumbs are evenly coated. Set aside.

Place the salmon fillets, skin side down, on a board. Generously brush the top of the fillets with mustard and then sprinkle generously with salt and pepper. Press the panko mixture thickly on top of the mustard on each salmon fillet. The mustard will help the panko adhere.

Heat the vegetable oil over medium-high heat in a 12-inch cast-iron skillet or large heavy, ovenproof pan. When the oil is very hot, add the salmon fillets, skin side down, and sear for 3 to 4 minutes, without turning, to brown the skin.

Transfer the pan to the hot oven for 5 to 7 minutes until the salmon is almost cooked and the panko is browned. Remove from the oven, cover with aluminum foil, and allow to rest for 5 to 10 minutes. Serve the salmon hot or at room temperature with lemon wedges.

weeknight bolognese

Everyone needs a quick dinner they can throw together during the week. Bolognese is a thick meat sauce that is a staple of northern Italy. It's always made with beef, tomatoes, and cream and I've added oregano, red pepper flakes, and basil to give it lots of flavor. It's the perfect stick-to-your-ribs dinner on a cold night.

2 tablespoons	good olive oil, plus extra to cook the pasta
1 pound	lean ground sirloin
4 teaspoons	minced garlic (4 cloves)
1 tablespoon	dried oregano
¼ teaspoon	crushed red pepper flakes
1¼ cups	dry red wine, divided
1	(28-ounce) can crushed tomatoes, preferably San Marzano
2 tablespoons	tomato paste
	Kosher salt and freshly ground black pepper
¾ pound	dried pasta, such as orecchiette or small shells
¼ teaspoon	ground nutmeg
¼ cup	chopped fresh basil leaves, lightly packed
¼ cup	heavy cream
½ cup	freshly grated Parmesan cheese, plus extra for serving

Heat 2 tablespoons of olive oil in a large (12-inch) skillet over medium-high heat. Add the ground sirloin and cook, crumbling the meat with a wooden spoon, for 5 to 7 minutes, until the meat has lost its pink color and has started to brown. Stir in the garlic, oregano, and red pepper flakes and cook for 1 more minute. Pour 1 cup of the wine into the skillet and stir to scrape up any browned bits. Add the tomatoes, tomato paste, 1 tablespoon salt, and 1½ teaspoons pepper, stirring until combined. Bring to a boil, lower the heat, and simmer for 10 minutes.

Meanwhile, bring a large pot of water to a boil, add a tablespoon of salt, a splash of oil, and the pasta, and cook according to the directions on the box.

While the pasta cooks, finish the sauce. Add the nutmeg, basil, cream, and the remaining ¼ cup wine to the sauce and simmer for 8 to 10 minutes, stirring occasionally until thickened. When the pasta is cooked, drain and pour into a large serving bowl. Add the sauce and ½ cup Parmesan and toss well. Serve hot with Parmesan on the side.

spaghetti aglio e olio

Spaghetti with garlic and olive oil has to be one of the easiest dinners ever. It's sometimes called Midnight Spaghetti because chefs make it for a quick meal at midnight when they get home from work. This has an amazing amount of garlic, but it gets sweeter when you cook it in the oil. The pasta is great on its own or dressed up for company with some roasted shrimp and broccoli.

	Kosher salt
1 pound	dried spaghetti, such as DeCecco
⅓ cup	good olive oil
8	large garlic cloves, cut into thin slivers
½ teaspoon	crushed red pepper flakes
½ cup	minced fresh parsley
1 cup	freshly grated Parmesan cheese, plus extra for serving

Bring a large pot of water to a boil. Add 2 tablespoons of salt and the pasta and cook according to the directions on the package. Set aside 1½ cups of the pasta cooking water before you drain the pasta.

Meanwhile, heat the olive oil over medium heat in a pot large enough to hold the pasta, such as a 12-inch sauté pan or a large, shallow pot. Add the garlic and cook for 2 minutes, stirring frequently, until it *just* begins to turn golden on the edges—don't overcook it! Add the red pepper flakes and cook for 30 seconds more. Carefully add the reserved pasta-cooking water to the garlic and oil and bring to a boil. Lower the heat, add 1 teaspoon of salt, and simmer for about 5 minutes, until the liquid is reduced by about a third.

Add the drained pasta to the garlic sauce and toss. Off the heat, add the parsley and Parmesan and toss well. Allow the pasta to rest off the heat for 5 minutes for the sauce to be absorbed. Taste for seasoning and serve warm with extra Parmesan on the side.

spicy turkey meatballs & spaghetti

SERVES 8

This recipe was inspired by Mario Batali, who I admire enormously. His New York City restaurant Babbo always knocks me out. Instead of rolling ordinary meatballs around in a pan of hot oil, these are made with turkey, sausage, prosciutto, and Asiago cheese, and they bake in the oven before going into the sauce. Who wouldn't love that? And they're also the best meatballs I've ever had!

3 cups	(1-inch diced) bread cubes from a round rustic bread, crusts removed
⅔ cup	whole milk
2 pounds	ground turkey (85% to 92% lean)
½ pound	sweet Italian pork sausage, casings removed
4 ounces	thinly sliced prosciutto, finely chopped (see note)
1 cup	freshly grated aged Asiago cheese (see note)
½ cup	minced fresh parsley
1 teaspoon	dried oregano
1 teaspoon	crushed red pepper flakes
	Kosher salt and freshly ground black pepper
3 tablespoons	good olive oil, plus extra for brushing the meatballs
2	extra-large eggs, lightly beaten
3	(24-ounce) jars good marinara sauce, such as Rao's
2 pounds	dried spaghetti, such as De Cecco
	Freshly grated Parmesan cheese, for serving

Be sure the hard rind is fully removed from the prosciutto. An inexperienced deli person can accidentally leave it on and it's impossible to eat.

Preheat the oven to 400 degrees. Line 2 sheet pans with parchment paper.

Place the bread in the bowl of a food processor fitted with the steel blade. Process until the bread is in medium crumbs. Transfer the crumbs to a small bowl and add the milk. Set aside for 5 minutes.

In a large mixing bowl, combine the turkey, sausage, prosciutto, bread mixture, Asiago, parsley, oregano, red pepper flakes, 1 tablespoon salt, and 1½ teaspoons pepper. Lightly combine the ingredients with your hands. Add the 3 tablespoons of olive oil and the eggs, and stir lightly with a fork to combine.

With your hands, lightly roll the mixture into 2-inch-round meatballs and place them on the prepared sheet pans. Brush the meatballs with olive oil. Bake for 35 to 40 minutes, until the tops are browned and the centers are completely cooked.

Pour the marinara sauce in a large, low pot, add the meatballs, and bring to a simmer.

Meanwhile, cook the spaghetti in a large pot of boiling salted water according to the directions on the package. Drain and place the spaghetti in individual bowls, and top with 3 meatballs and lots of sauce. Serve with Parmesan cheese on the side.

I "grate" the Asiago the way I "grate" Parmesan—in the food processor. Don't use the grating blade; instead, cut the cheese in chunks and process with the steel blade until finely ground.

easy parmesan "risotto"

SERVES 4 TO 6

While not technically a classic Italian risotto, this sure is easy. I found the process for this recipe in a book by Donna Hay, the wonderful cookbook writer from Australia. I make it with my homemade chicken stock, lots of freshly grated Parmesan, and frozen peas. Risotto in the oven? You have to make this to believe it!

1½ cups	Arborio rice
5 cups	simmering chicken stock, preferably homemade (page 181), divided
1 cup	freshly grated Parmesan cheese
½ cup	dry white wine
3 tablespoons	unsalted butter, diced
2 teaspoons	kosher salt
1 teaspoon	freshly ground black pepper
1 cup	frozen peas

Preheat the oven to 350 degrees.

Place the rice and 4 cups of the chicken stock in a Dutch oven, such as Le Creuset. Cover and bake for 45 minutes, until most of the liquid is absorbed and the rice is al dente. Remove from the oven, add the remaining cup of chicken stock, the Parmesan, wine, butter, salt, and pepper, and stir vigorously for 2 to 3 minutes, until the rice is thick and creamy. Add the peas and stir until heated through. Serve hot.

vegetables

roasted summer vegetables

scalloped tomatoes

garlic-roasted cauliflower

flat beans with pecorino

roasted butternut squash

tomatoes roasted with pesto

creamy parmesan polenta

sausage-stuffed mushrooms

rich celery root purée

potato basil purée

warm french lentils

roasted pear & apple sauce

couscous with toasted pine nuts

tuscan white beans

13

Post-it notes
for platters

14

Cake stands

serving dinner

A big part of keeping a meal easy is serving it in an easy way. Before I was in the food business, I would serve dinner the old-fashioned way. Everything was put into bowls and either arranged on a buffet or brought to the table and passed around for people to help themselves. Then one day, when Jeffrey and I lived in Washington, D.C., we came to New York and went to Lee Bailey's store at Bendel's. Sadly, it's no longer there but now you can find things he carried everywhere. Lee had huge white platters that made it possible to serve the entire main course from a single dish. Curious how that would work, I brought one home to Washington. The next time I had a party, I put the meat and vegetables all on one platter and voilà! It looked like a party! I've never gone back to the old style again. Now, instead of passing all those bowls, I arrange Greek Lamb with Yogurt Mint Sauce (page 131) down the middle of the platter, Tomatoes Roasted with Pesto (page 179) down one side, and Couscous with Toasted Pine Nuts (page 195) down the other. If it's just a few people, I'll serve everyone at the table; or if it's a big party, I'll serve it from a buffet in the kitchen or the sideboard in the dining room. It's easier to assemble, easier to serve, and when everyone goes home, there's only one platter to clean up!

And here are those Post-it notes again—I keep them with a big pen in a kitchen drawer. Before guests arrive, I have all the platters I'll need for the whole meal set out and I put a note on each one so I'll know which dish goes on which platter. I've said this before—but it's worth repeating—when the turkey is carved isn't the moment you want to remember that you broke the platter last Thanksgiving and you forgot to replace it. Dinner's served—and no stress!

roasted summer vegetables

SERVES 6

People think of roasting vegetables in the winter and grilling them in the summer, but I find roasting so much easier than standing over a hot grill and watching the vegetables burn. For twenty years we made huge platters of roasted vegetables at Barefoot Contessa, and they're good with almost any dinner. All the vegetables roast in twenty minutes, so you can cook them together on sheet pans.

2	medium zucchinis
1	red bell pepper, preferably Holland
1	yellow or orange bell pepper, preferably Holland
1	fennel bulb
1	small red onion
2 tablespoons	good olive oil
1 tablespoon	minced garlic (3 cloves)
1 teaspoon	kosher salt
½ teaspoon	freshly ground black pepper
4	sprigs fresh thyme

Preheat the oven to 375 degrees.

Trim the ends of the zucchinis and cut them diagonally in ¾-inch-thick slices. (The slices will seem large, but they'll shrink while they cook.) Cut the peppers lengthwise in 1½-inch-wide slices, discarding the core. Trim off the fennel stalks and cut the bulb through the core in 1-inch wedges. (Cutting through the core keeps the pieces intact.) Peel the onion and slice it in ¼-inch-thick rounds, leaving the slices intact.

Place the vegetables in groups on a sheet pan. Drizzle with the olive oil, add the garlic, and toss gently to be sure the vegetables are lightly coated with oil. Spread the vegetables in one layer on 2 sheet pans. (If they're crowded, they'll steam rather than roast.) Sprinkle with the salt and pepper and place the thyme sprigs on top. Roast for 15 minutes. Turn each piece and put the pans back in the oven for 5 to 10 minutes, until all the vegetables are crisp-tender. Sprinkle with extra salt and serve hot or at room temperature.

scalloped tomatoes

Sarah Chase is not only a dear friend, but she's also one of my cooking inspirations. Her food is delicious and always easy to make. The secrets to these scalloped tomatoes, inspired by a recipe in her book Cold Weather Cooking, *are first, that you can use grocery-store plum tomatoes, and second, that you can prepare the dish in advance and bake it before dinner. Great summer flavors— tomatoes, basil, and garlic—all year round!*

5 tablespoons	good olive oil, divided
2 cups	(½-inch) diced bread from a round rustic bread, crusts removed
3 pounds	plum tomatoes, ½-inch-diced (14 to 16 tomatoes)
1 tablespoon	minced garlic (3 cloves)
2 tablespoons	sugar
2 teaspoons	kosher salt
1 teaspoon	freshly ground black pepper
½ cup	julienned fresh basil leaves, lightly packed
1 cup	freshly grated Parmesan cheese

Preheat the oven to 350 degrees.

Heat 3 tablespoons of the olive oil in a large (12-inch) sauté pan over medium heat. Add the bread cubes and stir to coat with the oil. Cook over medium to medium-high heat for 5 minutes, stirring often, until the cubes are evenly browned.

Meanwhile, combine the tomatoes, garlic, sugar, salt, and pepper in a large bowl. Add the tomato mixture to the bread cubes and continue to cook over medium-high heat, stirring often, for 5 minutes. Off the heat, stir in the basil.

Pour the tomato mixture into a shallow (6- to 8-cup) baking dish. Sprinkle evenly with the Parmesan cheese and drizzle with the remaining 2 tablespoons of olive oil. Bake for 35 to 40 minutes until the top is browned and the tomatoes are bubbly. Serve hot or warm.

garlic-roasted cauliflower

*This recipe is surprising in so many ways. First, who thinks of cauliflower
as flavorful? Second, roasting all that garlic in olive oil makes it delicious. And
third, it's so easy! Roast the cauliflower with the garlic and then toss it with
toasted pine nuts, parsley, and fresh lemon juice. You'll never think cauliflower is
boring again.*

1	whole head of garlic, cloves separated but not peeled
1	large head of cauliflower, trimmed and cut into large florets (see note)
4½ tablespoons	good olive oil, divided
	Kosher salt and freshly ground black pepper
¼ cup	minced fresh parsley
3 tablespoons	pine nuts, toasted (page 195)
2 tablespoons	freshly squeezed lemon juice

*If I can't find
a large head,
I buy 2 small heads
of cauliflower.*

Preheat the oven to 450 degrees.

Bring a small pot of water to a boil and add the garlic cloves. Boil
for 15 seconds. Drain, peel, and cut off any brown parts. Cut the
largest cloves in half lengthwise.

On a sheet pan, toss the cauliflower with the garlic, 3 tablespoons
of the olive oil, 2 teaspoons salt, and 1 teaspoon pepper. Spread the
mixture out in a single layer and roast for 20 to 25 minutes, tossing
twice, until the cauliflower is tender and the garlic is lightly
browned.

Scrape the cauliflower into a large bowl with the garlic and pan
juices. Add the remaining 1½ tablespoons olive oil, the parsley, pine
nuts, and lemon juice. Sprinkle with another ½ teaspoon of salt,
toss well, and serve hot or warm.

flat beans with pecorino

SERVES 6

There's a wonderful farm behind the Amagansett Farmers Market called Amber Waves. If you belong to its Community Supported Agriculture group, you get the most beautiful basket of produce every week. I found these broad beans in my basket one day and I had no idea what to do with them. Katie and Amanda, the farmers, suggested that I boil them for three minutes and drizzle them with olive oil. I added a shaving of Pecorino—they were so simple and delicious! Be sure you buy young beans or they can be very tough.

	Kosher salt
1½ pounds	fresh Romano or flat beans, trimmed
1½ tablespoons	good olive oil
1½ teaspoons	sea salt or fleur de sel
¾ teaspoon	freshly ground black pepper
4 to 5 ounces	shaved aged Pecorino Romano cheese

I shave the Pecorino with a vegetable peeler.

Bring a large pot of water to a boil, add a tablespoon of salt and the flat beans, and cook for 3 minutes, or until the beans are just tender. Drain immediately and place the beans on a platter. Drizzle with the olive oil and sprinkle with the sea salt and pepper. Toss with the Pecorino and serve hot or warm.

roasted butternut squash

I love butternut squash in any form. When I'm in a hurry, though, this is about as easy as it gets. You can cut the squash a day or two in advance and throw it into the oven before dinner. It's a simple winter dish that's great served with Herb-Roasted Turkey Breast (page 127) and mashed potatoes.

1 large	(4-pound) butternut squash, peeled, seeded, and 1-inch-diced
3 tablespoons	good olive oil
1 tablespoon	minced fresh thyme leaves
2 teaspoons	kosher salt
1 teaspoon	freshly ground black pepper

Preheat the oven to 400 degrees.

Place the squash on a sheet pan, add the olive oil, thyme, salt, and pepper, and toss with your hands. Roast for 30 to 40 minutes, until tender, tossing once during cooking with a large metal spatula so the cubes brown evenly. Season to taste and serve hot.

tomatoes roasted with pesto

SERVES 6

This is a very flavorful tomato dish made with garlicky pesto, so it needs a quiet partner on the plate—like roasted fish—to balance it. It's a wonderful way to give boring grocery-store tomatoes that delicious summer tomato flavor. I freeze extra pesto in small batches so I always have some on hand.

2 to 2½ pounds	large red tomatoes (see note)
3 tablespoons	good olive oil
2 teaspoons	dried oregano
	Kosher salt
½ teaspoon	freshly ground black pepper
½ cup	pesto, store-bought or homemade (recipe follows)
½ cup	freshly grated Parmesan cheese

Because these tomatoes are roasted, I choose firm ripe tomatoes. Heirloom tomatoes fall apart when they're roasted, so they're best served fresh in a salad.

Preheat the oven to 425 degrees.

Core the tomatoes and then slice them across (not through the stem) in ½-inch-thick slices. Arrange the slices in a single layer on a sheet pan. Drizzle the tomatoes with the olive oil and sprinkle with the oregano, 1½ teaspoons salt, and the pepper.

Bake the tomatoes for 10 minutes. Remove them from the oven, spread each slice with pesto, and sprinkle with the Parmesan cheese. Return the tomatoes to the oven and continue baking for 7 to 10 minutes, until the Parmesan is melted and begins to brown. Using a flat metal spatula, put the tomatoes on a serving platter, sprinkle with extra salt, and serve hot, warm, or at room temperature.

pesto

¼ cup	walnuts
¼ cup	pine nuts
3 tablespoons	diced garlic (9 cloves)
5 cups	fresh basil leaves, packed
1 teaspoon	kosher salt
1 teaspoon	freshly ground black pepper
1½ cups	good olive oil
1 cup	freshly grated Parmesan cheese

Place the walnuts, pine nuts, and garlic in the bowl of a food processor fitted with the steel blade. Process for 30 seconds. Add the basil, salt, and pepper. With the processor running, slowly pour the olive oil into the bowl through the feed tube and process until the pesto is puréed. Add the Parmesan and purée for a minute. Use immediately or store the pesto in the refrigerator or freezer with a thin film of olive oil on top.

To clean basil, remove the leaves from the stems, swirl them in a bowl of water, and then spin them very dry in a salad spinner. Store them in a closed plastic bag with a slightly damp paper towel. As long as the leaves are dry they will stay green for several days.

homemade chicken stock

3	(5-pound) roasting chickens
3	large yellow onions, unpeeled, quartered
6	carrots, unpeeled, halved
4	celery stalks with leaves, cut in thirds
4	parsnips, unpeeled, cut in half (optional)
20	sprigs fresh parsley
15	sprigs fresh thyme
20	sprigs fresh dill
1	head garlic, unpeeled, cut in half crosswise
2 tablespoons	kosher salt
2 teaspoons	whole black peppercorns

Place the chickens, onions, carrots, celery, parsnips, parsley, thyme, dill, garlic, salt, and peppercorns in a 16- to 20-quart stockpot. Add 7 quarts of water and bring to a boil. Simmer uncovered for 4 hours. Strain the entire contents of the pot through a colander and discard the solids. Pack in quart containers and chill overnight. Refrigerate for up to 5 days or freeze for up to 3 months.

creamy parmesan polenta

SERVES 6

This is my idea of heaven—it's like cream of wheat cereal but with flavor. I love to serve it with pan-roasted chicken sausages—it's the side dish that becomes the star of the meal.

4 cups	chicken stock, preferably homemade (page 181)
2 teaspoons	minced garlic (2 cloves)
1 cup	yellow cornmeal, preferably stone-ground (see note)
1 tablespoon	kosher salt
1 teaspoon	freshly ground black pepper
1 cup	freshly grated Parmesan cheese, plus extra for serving
¼ cup	crème fraîche
2 tablespoons	(¼ stick) unsalted butter

Place the chicken stock in a large saucepan. Add the garlic and cook over medium-high heat until the stock comes to a boil. Reduce the heat to medium-low and very slowly whisk in the cornmeal, whisking constantly to make sure there are no lumps. Switch to a wooden spoon, add the salt and pepper, and simmer, stirring almost constantly, for 10 minutes, until thick. Be sure to scrape the bottom of the pan thoroughly while you're stirring. Off the heat, stir in the Parmesan, crème fraîche, and butter. Taste for seasonings and serve hot with extra Parmesan cheese to sprinkle on top.

I use Quaker yellow cornmeal or Indian Head stone-ground cornmeal. If you have a choice, use "medium" rather than coarse or fine.

To reheat the polenta, place the cold mixture in a pot with extra chicken stock or water and reheat slowly over low heat, stirring until smooth.

sausage-stuffed mushrooms

SERVES 6 TO 8

*When I'm making a turkey for Thanksgiving, I don't stuff it for two reasons.
First, I prefer stuffing that's crunchy outside and moist inside rather than the
soggy stuffing that comes out of the bird. Second, in order for the stuffing to be
done, the turkey has to cook longer and it ends up being dry. My solution? I roast
a turkey and make these mushrooms filled with sausage-and-bread stuffing to
serve alongside.*

16	extra-large white mushrooms, caps and stems separated
5 tablespoons	good olive oil, divided
2½ tablespoons	Marsala wine or medium-dry sherry
¾ pound	sweet Italian sausage, casings removed
¾ cup	minced scallions, white and green parts (6 scallions)
2 teaspoons	minced garlic (2 cloves)
1 teaspoon	kosher salt
½ teaspoon	freshly ground black pepper
⅔ cup	panko (Japanese dried bread flakes)
5 ounces	Italian mascarpone cheese
⅓ cup	freshly grated Parmesan cheese
2½ tablespoons	minced fresh parsley

Preheat the oven to 325 degrees.

Trim the mushroom stems and chop them finely. Set aside. Place
the mushroom caps in a shallow bowl and toss with 3 tablespoons
of the olive oil and the Marsala. Set aside.

Heat the remaining 2 tablespoons of olive oil in a medium skillet
over medium heat. Add the sausage, crumbling it with a wooden
spoon. Cook the sausage for 8 to 10 minutes, stirring frequently,
until it's completely browned. Add the chopped mushroom stems
and cook for 3 more minutes. Stir in the scallions, garlic, salt,
and pepper and cook for another 2 to 3 minutes, stirring occasionally. Add the panko crumbs, stirring to combine with the other

ingredients. Finally, swirl in the mascarpone and continue cooking until the mascarpone has melted and made the mixture creamy. Off the heat, stir in the Parmesan and parsley and season to taste. Cool slightly.

Fill each mushroom generously with the sausage mixture. Arrange the mushrooms in a baking dish large enough to hold them all in a snug single layer. Bake for 50 minutes, until the stuffing is browned and crusty.

rich celery root purée

SERVES 6 TO 8

This is the essence of simplicity, celery root enriched with chicken stock and cream so that all you taste is that fresh celery root flavor. I serve this with a simple roast pork and a bottle of full-bodied Chardonnay; I'm in heaven. You can easily make this a day in advance and reheat it before dinner.

5 pounds	celery root (2 large)
2 tablespoons	unsalted butter
1½ cups	chicken stock, preferably homemade (page 181)
1½ cups	heavy cream
4 teaspoons	kosher salt
1 teaspoon	freshly ground black pepper

Peel the celery roots with a large chef's knife and cut each one in half. With the cut side down, cut it in ½-inch dice, removing any brown spots. Be careful—keep your fingers out of the way of the knife!

Melt the butter in a large heavy-bottomed pot over medium-high heat. Add the celery root and sauté for 3 minutes, stirring to coat with the butter. Reduce the heat to medium-low, cover the pan, and cook for 10 minutes. Add the chicken stock, cream, salt, and pepper and bring to a boil. Lower the heat, cover, and simmer for 15 to 20 minutes, stirring once, until the celery root is very tender.

In batches, transfer the mixture to a food processor fitted with the steel blade and purée until smooth. Return the purée to the pot and reheat gently over low heat. Check the seasonings—it should be very highly seasoned—and serve hot.

Celery root looks ugly, but it's delicious!

potato basil purée

There are so many variations on mashed potatoes—but this combination of potatoes and basil is a marriage made in heaven. Creamy potatoes and the fresh peppery basil really complement each other, and the Parmesan doesn't hurt, either. Everyone asks for seconds!

2 cups	fresh basil leaves, lightly packed
2 pounds	large Yukon Gold or white boiling potatoes
1 cup	half-and-half
¾ cup	freshly grated Parmesan cheese, plus extra for serving
2 teaspoons	kosher salt
1 teaspoon	freshly ground black pepper

Bring a large pot of salted water to a rolling boil and fill a bowl with ice water. Add the basil leaves to the boiling water and cook for exactly 15 seconds. Remove the basil with a slotted spoon and immediately plunge the leaves into the ice water to set the bright green color. Drain and set aside.

Peel the potatoes and cut them in quarters. Add the potatoes to the same pot of boiling water and return to a boil. Cook the potatoes for 20 to 25 minutes, until very tender. Drain well, return to the sauce-pan, and steam over low heat until any remaining water evaporates.

In a small saucepan over medium heat, heat the half-and-half and Parmesan cheese until the cream simmers. Place the basil in a food processor fitted with the steel blade and purée. Add the hot cream mixture and process until smooth.

With a handheld mixer with the beater attachment, beat the hot potatoes in the pot until they are broken up. Slowly add the hot basil cream, the salt, and pepper and beat until smooth. If the potatoes need to be reheated, cover and cook gently over low heat for a few minutes. Pour into a serving bowl, sprinkle with extra Parmesan cheese, season to taste, and serve hot.

warm french lentils

There's a little bistro in Paris that Jeffrey and I love and they always have lentils on the menu. In summer, they're served like this—slightly warm with a drizzle of olive oil—and in winter they're served hot with garlicky French sausages. This is classic French peasant food and it's so satisfying.

2 tablespoons	plus ¼ cup good olive oil
1	leek, white and light green parts, sliced ¼ inch thick
2	carrots, scrubbed and ½-inch-diced
1 teaspoon	minced garlic
1 cup	French green Le Puy lentils
1	whole onion, peeled and stuck with 6 whole cloves
1	white turnip, cut in half
1 teaspoon	unsalted butter
4 teaspoons	Dijon mustard
2 tablespoons	red wine vinegar
1 tablespoon	kosher salt
1 teaspoon	freshly ground black pepper

Heat the 2 tablespoons of olive oil in a medium sauté pan, add the leek and carrots, and cook over medium heat for 5 minutes. Add the garlic and cook for 1 more minute and set aside.

Meanwhile, place the lentils, 4 cups of water, the onion with the cloves, and the turnip in a large saucepan and bring to a boil. Lower the heat, add the leek and carrots, and simmer uncovered for 20 minutes, or until the lentils are almost tender. Remove and discard the onion and turnip and drain the lentils. Place them in a medium bowl and add the butter.

Meanwhile, whisk together the ¼ cup of olive oil, the mustard, vinegar, salt, and pepper. Add to the lentils, stir well, and allow the lentils to cool until just warm, about 15 minutes. Sprinkle with salt and pepper and serve. The longer the lentils sit, the more salt and pepper you'll want to add.

roasted pear & apple sauce

MAKES 2 QUARTS

My friend Brent Newsom makes a delicious roasted applesauce that I love to make when the apples arrive at the farmstands in East Hampton. Once I had some extra pears, which I threw into the pot, and discovered an even better recipe! This is delicious served as a side dish with chicken or turkey, but it's also good served warm for dessert with a drizzle of half-and-half or a scoop of vanilla ice cream.

Bosc pears are ripe when they turn from green to brown, but they'll still be hard.

You can use a grater or zester for the citrus, but I prefer a strip zester because I like to see strips of zest in the finished applesauce.

	Zest and juice of 2 large navel oranges
	Zest and juice of 1 lemon
3 pounds	sweet red apples, such as Macoun or Empire (8 apples)
3 pounds	ripe Bosc pears (7 pears)
½ cup	light brown sugar, lightly packed
2 tablespoons	unsalted butter
1 teaspoon	ground cinnamon

Preheat the oven to 350 degrees.

Place the zest and juice of the oranges and lemon in a nonreactive Dutch oven such as Le Creuset. Peel, quarter, and core the apples and pears and toss them in the juice. Add the brown sugar, butter, and cinnamon and cover the pot. Bake for 1¼ to 1½ hours, until the apples and pears are tender. Mix with a whisk until the applesauce is smooth but still a little chunky. Depending on the ripeness of the fruit, the apples will likely fall apart and the pears will break up but stay chunky. Serve warm or at room temperature.

couscous with toasted pine nuts

SERVES 6 TO 8

If you can boil a pot of water, you can make couscous. To make my life easy when I'm entertaining, I sauté the onions, add the stock, salt, and pepper and set it aside. Before dinner, all I have to do is heat the stock, add the couscous, and wait ten minutes for a delicious side dish with no stress.

4 tablespoons	(½ stick) unsalted butter
2 cups	chopped yellow onion (2 onions)
3 cups	chicken stock, preferably homemade (page 181)
1½ teaspoons	kosher salt
½ teaspoon	freshly ground black pepper
2 cups	couscous (12 ounces)
½ cup	pine nuts, toasted (see note)
½ cup	minced fresh parsley

Melt the butter in a large saucepan. Add the onion and cook over medium-low heat for 8 to 10 minutes, stirring occasionally, until tender but not browned. Add the chicken stock, salt, and pepper and bring to a full boil. Stir in the couscous, turn off the heat, cover, and allow to steam for 10 minutes. Fluff with a fork, stir in the pine nuts and parsley, and serve hot.

To toast pine nuts, place them in a dry sauté pan and cook over low heat for 10 minutes, tossing often, until lightly browned.

tuscan white beans

SERVES 6

In Tuscany, white beans are served instead of rice or mashed potatoes with the main course, but I've also served these creamy beans as a first course on slices of grilled bread and drizzled with olive oil. This dish tastes best when made with dried beans, but they do need to soak overnight. I cook them with fennel, carrots, garlic, and chicken stock plus lots of fresh rosemary and sage. Pecorino added at the end not only flavors the sauce but thickens it as well.

1 pound	dried white cannellini beans
¼ cup	good olive oil
4 cups	chopped fennel, stalks, fronds, and core removed (2 large)
2 cups	chopped carrots (4 carrots)
1 tablespoon	minced garlic (3 cloves)
1 cup	chicken stock, preferably homemade (page 181)
1 tablespoon	minced fresh sage leaves
1 tablespoon	minced fresh rosemary leaves
2 teaspoons	kosher salt
½ teaspoon	freshly ground black pepper
½ cup	freshly grated Pecorino Romano cheese

Don't add salt or anything acidic to beans while they boil; it makes the skins tough.

The night before, soak the beans in a large bowl with water to cover by at least 2 inches. Cover and refrigerate overnight.

The next day, drain the beans, rinse them well, and place them in a large stockpot. Add twice as much water as you have beans, bring to a boil, lower the heat, and simmer uncovered for about 45 minutes, until the beans are very tender. Skim off any foam that accumulates.

Meanwhile, heat the olive oil in a large pan or Dutch oven over medium heat. Add the fennel and carrots and sauté for 8 to 10 minutes, stirring occasionally, until tender. Add the garlic and cook for 1 minute more. Drain the beans and add them to the vegetables. Add the chicken stock, sage, rosemary, salt, and pepper and simmer, stirring occasionally, for 12 to 15 minutes, until creamy. Stir in the Pecorino, season to taste, and serve hot.

desserts

ultimate peach ice cream, page 276

easy cranberry & apple cake

mocha chocolate icebox cake

roasted figs with caramel sauce

chocolate pudding cream tart

eton mess

strawberry rhubarb crisp

fresh peach cake

italian plum tart

red velvet cupcakes

rum raisin tiramisù

old-fashioned banana cake

strawberry shortcakes, deconstructed

ultimate peach ice cream

chocolate hazelnut cookies

new york egg cream

fleur de sel caramels

white chocolate bark

15

Extra mixing bowls

16

Cake testers

baking tips

I've often said that there are two kinds of people in this world: cooks and bakers. Cooks love to toss things into a pan and see what happens. Bakers tend to be precise. You can't throw a handful of flour into a cake and see what happens; it needs to be lightened, placed carefully in a dry measuring cup, and leveled off with a spatula or knife. I don't have a million pieces of baking equipment, just the ones that give me the confidence that my baked goods will come out perfectly every time.

Most of all, I love my KitchenAid mixer. Sure, I could have bought a less expensive mixer, but this is a great investment that will last forever. You can certainly bake everything in this book with a handheld mixer—but instead of standing there holding a mixer, I'd much rather be prepping the rest of the ingredients for my cake.

A few key pieces of equipment make all the difference. First, I prefer a French rolling pin because I can really *feel* the dough while I'm rolling it out. Second, I have three timers on the stove so I can have several things baking at once—and I won't forget about them! Next is a digital scale; if a package of chocolate chips is 12 ounces and I need only 6, a scale ensures that my quantities are accurate. Finally, I have lots of thermometers—oven thermometers, candy thermometers, and instant-read thermometers—so I know when something is exactly the right temperature.

There are also some time-saving techniques. I have stacks of sheet pans and lots of parchment paper nearby. There's no point in making delicious cookies if you can't get them off the pan—and then cleanup is a snap! And if all else fails—I have Plan B. I keep lots of great mixes in the pantry for last-minute baking. In a pinch, I can treat my guests to delicious desserts and they never need to know it only took me fifteen minutes to whip them up.

easy cranberry & apple cake

SERVES 6 TO 8

This recipe is inspired by a cranberry pie from Sarah Chase's book Cold Weather Cooking. *My friend Barbara Liberman calls it "easy cake"—I call it delicious. It's even better served warm with vanilla ice cream.*

12 ounces	fresh cranberries, rinsed and picked over for stems
1	Granny Smith apple, peeled, cored, and diced
½ cup	light brown sugar, lightly packed
1 tablespoon	grated orange zest (2 oranges)
¼ cup	freshly squeezed orange juice
1⅛ teaspoons	ground cinnamon, divided
2	extra-large eggs, at room temperature
1 cup	plus 1 tablespoon granulated sugar
¼ pound	(1 stick) unsalted butter, melted and slightly cooled
1 teaspoon	pure vanilla extract
¼ cup	sour cream
1 cup	all-purpose flour
¼ teaspoon	kosher salt

Preheat the oven to 325 degrees.

Combine the cranberries, apple, brown sugar, orange zest, orange juice, and 1 teaspoon of the cinnamon in a medium bowl. Set aside.

In the bowl of an electric mixer fitted with the paddle attachment, beat the eggs on medium-high speed for 2 minutes. With the mixer on medium, add 1 cup of the granulated sugar, the butter, vanilla, and sour cream and beat just until combined. On low speed, slowly add the flour and salt.

Pour the fruit mixture evenly into a 10-inch glass pie plate. Pour the batter over the fruit, covering it completely. Combine the remaining 1 tablespoon of granulated sugar and ⅛ teaspoon of cinnamon and sprinkle it over the batter. Bake for 55 to 60 minutes, until a toothpick inserted in the middle of the cake comes out clean and the fruit is bubbling around the edges. Serve warm or at room temperature.

mocha chocolate icebox cake

SERVES 8

Almost everyone has fond memories of that old-fashioned dessert made with chocolate wafers and whipped cream. I decided to update that icebox cake with really good chocolate chip cookies and mocha whipped cream. WOW—and talk about easy! I use chocolate chip cookies from Tate's Bake Shop in Southampton, New York, which are available nationally or at TatesBakeShop.com. If you can't get them, use another thin, crisp chocolate chip cookie.

Tate's Bake Shop cookies are 2 inches in diameter, thin, and crisp. You will have cookies left over from 3 packages, which never seems to be a problem here.

If you heat the block of chocolate in a microwave for 30 seconds, you will get larger shavings.

2 cups	cold heavy cream
12 ounces	Italian mascarpone cheese
½ cup	sugar
¼ cup	Kahlúa liqueur
2 tablespoons	unsweetened cocoa powder, such as Pernigotti
1 teaspoon	instant espresso powder
1 teaspoon	pure vanilla extract
3	(8-ounce) packages Tate's Bake Shop chocolate chip cookies
	Shaved semisweet chocolate, for garnish

In the bowl of an electric mixer fitted with the whisk attachment, combine the heavy cream, mascarpone, sugar, Kahlúa, cocoa powder, espresso powder, and vanilla. Mix on low speed to combine and then slowly raise the speed, until it forms firm peaks.

To assemble the cake, arrange chocolate chip cookies flat in an 8-inch springform pan, covering the bottom as much as possible. (I break some cookies to fill in the spaces.) Spread a fifth of the mocha whipped cream evenly over the cookies. Place another layer of cookies on top, lying flat and touching, followed by another fifth of the cream. Continue layering cookies and cream until there are 5 layers of each, ending with a layer of cream. Smooth the top, cover with plastic wrap, and refrigerate overnight.

Run a small sharp knife around the outside of the cake and remove the sides of the pan. Sprinkle the top with the chocolate, cut in wedges, and serve cold.

roasted figs with caramel sauce

SERVES 8

My friend Frank Newbold told me that he'd been served fresh figs with caramel sauce at a friend's house. Roasting the figs makes them even sweeter. I make my own caramel, but you can make this dessert even easier by using store-bought sauce such as Fran's. The sweetness of the figs balances the burnt sugar of the caramel plus the crunch of toasted almonds. It's simple but impressive.

1½ cups	sugar
1¼ cups	heavy cream
½ teaspoon	pure vanilla extract
24 to 30	large fresh black figs (page 28)
6 tablespoons	sliced almonds, toasted (see note)

Mix ⅓ cup of water and the sugar in a medium heavy-bottomed saucepan. Cook without stirring over low heat for 5 to 10 minutes, until the sugar dissolves. Increase the heat to medium and boil uncovered for 5 to 7 minutes, until the sugar turns a warm chestnut brown (350 degrees on a candy thermometer), gently swirling the pan to stir the mixture. Be careful—the melted sugar is hot! Watch the mixture constantly at the end, as it will go from caramel to burnt very quickly. Turn off the heat. Stand back to avoid splattering and slowly add the cream and vanilla. The cream will bubble violently and the caramel will solidify; don't worry. Simmer over low heat, stirring constantly, until the caramel dissolves and the sauce is smooth, about 2 minutes. Allow to cool to room temperature, at least 4 hours. It will thicken as it sits. Store at room temperature.

Preheat the oven to 450 degrees. Place a wire baking rack on a sheet pan.

Cut the hard stem off each fig and cut each one in half through the stem. Place all the halves cut side up on the baking rack. Roast the figs for 10 minutes, until they're tender.

When the figs are done, heat the caramel sauce (I do it in a microwave) just until warm. Place the figs in dessert bowls, drizzle each serving with a tablespoon of caramel sauce, and sprinkle with the almonds. Serve warm.

To toast nuts, place them in a small dry sauté pan and cook over low heat for 5 to 10 minutes, tossing often, until evenly browned.

To make in advance, cut the figs and place them on the wire baking rack. Ten minutes before serving, put the figs in the oven and warm the caramel sauce.

chocolate pudding cream tart

SERVES 8

This is an old-fashioned dessert that we used to make at Barefoot Contessa—basically, it's a rich chocolate pudding dressed up in a tart pan. I use bittersweet Lindt chocolate and then flavor the pudding with coffee and Kahlúa. You don't know the coffee is in there but it makes the chocolate better.

for the crust

2 cups	graham cracker crumbs (see note)
⅓ cup	sugar
¼ pound	(1 stick) unsalted butter, melted

for the filling

4 cups	whole milk
¾ cup	sugar
5	extra-large egg yolks
⅓ cup	cornstarch
1 teaspoon	kosher salt
7 ounces	good bittersweet chocolate, such as Lindt, broken
2 tablespoons	(¼ stick) unsalted butter, diced
1 tablespoon	Kahlúa liqueur
1 teaspoon	instant coffee powder, such as Nescafé Clásico
	Sweetened whipped cream (see note)
	Shaved bittersweet chocolate, for garnish

To make 2 cups of graham cracker crumbs, crush 14 graham crackers into a food processor fitted with the steel blade and process until finely ground.

Preheat the oven to 350 degrees.

Combine the graham crackers, sugar, and butter in a bowl and mix well with a wooden spoon. Lightly press the mixture into an 11-inch metal tart pan with removable sides. Bake for 10 minutes and set aside to cool.

Heat the milk in a small saucepan until almost simmering. In the bowl of an electric mixer fitted with the paddle attachment, combine the sugar, egg yolks, cornstarch, and salt and, with the mixer on low speed, slowly pour the milk into the bowl. (I pour the hot milk into a large measuring cup first to reduce spills.) Pour the mixture into a large saucepan and cook over medium-low heat for 5 to 10 minutes, stirring constantly with a wooden spoon, until the mixture is very thick. Off the heat, add the chocolate, butter, Kahlúa, and coffee. Beat with a whisk until smooth and pour into the cooled crust. Place plastic wrap directly on the chocolate filling and chill the tart for 6 hours, until cold. Decorate with whipped cream and shaved chocolate and serve cold.

To make sweetened whipped cream, place 1 cup heavy cream, 2 tablespoons sugar, and 1 teaspoon pure vanilla extract in the bowl of an electric mixer fitted with the whisk attachment. Beat until it forms firm peaks.

eton mess

Eton mess is an English boarding school dessert that incorporates several of my favorite things—fruit, whipped cream, and meringue—all smooshed together. If it's made with raspberries and served in beautiful glasses, it's also a very elegant dessert. I cook the raspberries in advance and then assemble the glasses before the party.

I buy meringues from a bakery and store them in a sealed plastic bag at room temperature to keep them very dry.

4	(6-ounce) packages fresh raspberries, divided
1 cup	plus 3 tablespoons sugar
1 tablespoon	freshly squeezed lemon juice
1 tablespoon	framboise liqueur
1½ cups	cold heavy cream
1 teaspoon	pure vanilla extract
3	(3-inch) bakery meringue shells, broken in pieces

Pour 2 packages of the raspberries, 1 cup of sugar, and the lemon juice into a 10-inch sauté pan. Crush the berries lightly with a fork and bring the mixture to a full boil over medium-high heat. Lower the heat and simmer for 10 minutes, stirring occasionally, until the mixture is syrupy. Fold the remaining 2 packages of raspberries and the framboise into the hot mixture and refrigerate until very cold.

In the bowl of an electric mixer fitted with the whisk attachment, beat the cream, the remaining 3 tablespoons of sugar, and the vanilla together on medium-high speed until it forms firm peaks.

In decorative glasses, layer a spoonful of the whipped cream, a spoonful of the raspberry mixture, and then a few meringue pieces. Repeat once or twice, depending on the size of the glasses, until the glasses are full, ending with berries and a dollop of cream. Serve immediately or chill for an hour, until ready to serve.

strawberry rhubarb crisp

SERVES 6

A friend called one day to say she'd been given some rhubarb and wanted to make a crisp. Could I help? Truth is, I'd never made one myself but this kind of dessert is so simple to make that I just talked her through it. The key is to add enough orange and sugar to enhance the rhubarb without overpowering the flavor of the strawberries. Put it in the oven right before guests arrive and the house will smell great.

The amount of cornstarch you add depends on the juiciness of the berries and the ripeness of the rhubarb. Green rhubarb has more pectin, so the juices will set better. This is delicious any way it comes out!

4 cups	fresh rhubarb, 1-inch diced (4 to 5 stalks)
4 cups	fresh strawberries, hulled and halved, if large
1¼ cups	granulated sugar, divided
1½ teaspoons	grated orange zest
1 tablespoon	cornstarch (see note)
½ cup	freshly squeezed orange juice
1 cup	all-purpose flour
½ cup	light brown sugar, lightly packed
½ teaspoon	kosher salt
1 cup	quick-cooking (not instant) oatmeal, such as McCann's
12 tablespoons	(1½ sticks) cold unsalted butter, diced
	Vanilla ice cream, for serving

Preheat the oven to 350 degrees.

For the fruit, toss the rhubarb, strawberries, ¾ cup granulated sugar, and the orange zest together in a large bowl. In a measuring cup, dissolve the cornstarch in the orange juice and then mix it into the fruit. Pour the mixture into an 8 × 11-inch baking dish and place it on a sheet pan lined with parchment paper.

For the topping, in the bowl of an electric mixer fitted with the paddle attachment, combine the flour, the remaining ½ cup granulated sugar, the brown sugar, salt, and oatmeal. With the mixer on low speed, add the butter and mix until the dry ingredients are moist and the mixture is in crumbles. Sprinkle the topping over the fruit, covering it completely, and bake for 1 hour, until the fruit is bubbling and the topping is golden brown. Serve warm with ice cream.

fresh peach cake

SERVES 8

This rich cake with fresh peaches is delicious served warm with a scoop of ice cream, but it's also good as a coffee cake for a special breakfast. It makes the house smell like cinnamon and sugar.

¼ pound	(1 stick) unsalted butter, at room temperature
1½ cups	sugar, divided
2	extra-large eggs, at room temperature
1 cup	sour cream, at room temperature
1 teaspoon	pure vanilla extract
2 cups	all-purpose flour
1 teaspoon	baking soda
1 teaspoon	baking powder
½ teaspoon	kosher salt
1 teaspoon	ground cinnamon
3	large, ripe peaches, peeled, pitted, and sliced
½ cup	chopped pecans

You can make this recipe even easier; substitute 16 ounces frozen peaches, defrosted.

Preheat the oven to 350 degrees. Grease a 9-inch square baking pan.

In the bowl of an electric mixer fitted with the paddle attachment, beat the butter and 1 cup of the sugar for 3 to 5 minutes on medium-high speed, until light and fluffy. With the mixer on low, add the eggs, one at a time, then the sour cream and vanilla, and mix until the batter is smooth. In a separate bowl, sift together the flour, baking soda, baking powder, and salt. With the mixer on low, slowly add the dry ingredients to the batter and mix just until combined. In a small bowl, combine the remaining ½ cup sugar and the cinnamon.

Spread half of the batter evenly in the pan. Top with half of the peaches, then sprinkle with two-thirds of the sugar mixture. Spread the remaining batter on top, arrange the remaining peaches on top, and sprinkle with the remaining sugar mixture and the pecans.

Bake the cake for 45 to 55 minutes, until a toothpick inserted in the center comes out clean. Serve warm or at room temperature.

italian plum tart

SERVES 8

Plums are easy to make into tarts because they don't have to be peeled like apples or pears. Sadly, Italian prune plums are only available in September and October, but they're worth waiting for.

¾ pound	Italian prune plums, quartered and pitted
2 tablespoons	Minute tapioca
2 tablespoons	crème de cassis liqueur
1¾ cups	sugar, divided
¼ pound	(1 stick) unsalted butter, at room temperature
1¼ cups	all-purpose flour
½ teaspoon	ground cinnamon
½ teaspoon	kosher salt
¼ teaspoon	baking powder

Preheat the oven to 350 degrees. Butter and flour a 9-inch spring-form pan and place it on a sheet pan.

Place the plums, tapioca, crème de cassis, and ¾ cup of the sugar in a mixing bowl and stir to combine. Allow to sit for 15 minutes.

In the bowl of an electric mixer fitted with the paddle attachment, cream the butter and remaining 1 cup of sugar on medium speed until light and fluffy. In a small bowl, combine the flour, cinnamon, salt, and baking powder. With the mixer on low, gradually add the dry ingredients to the butter mixture until it forms small, dry crumbs. Add 1 tablespoon of cold water and continue to beat for about 30 seconds, until the mixture forms large, moist crumbs. Set aside ¾ cup of the crumb mixture and pour the rest into the spring-form pan. With floured hands, lightly pat the dough evenly in the bottom of the pan and 1 inch up the sides.

Arrange the plums in concentric circles on the crust. Sprinkle the remaining crumb mixture evenly on top. Bake for 1 hour, until the fruit is bubbling and the crust is golden. Cool for 15 minutes, then remove the sides of the pan and serve warm or at room temperature.

red velvet cupcakes

MAKES 15 CUPCAKES

For my birthday, my friend Susan Stroman served an enormous red velvet cake and everyone went crazy! Rich chocolate cake and creamy frosting—perfect!

2½ cups	all-purpose flour
¼ cup	unsweetened cocoa powder, such as Pernigotti
1 teaspoon	baking powder
1 teaspoon	baking soda
1 teaspoon	kosher salt
1 cup	buttermilk, shaken
1 tablespoon	liquid red food coloring
1 teaspoon	white vinegar
1 teaspoon	pure vanilla extract
¼ pound	(1 stick) unsalted butter, at room temperature
1½ cups	sugar
2	extra-large eggs, at room temperature
	Red Velvet Frosting (recipe follows)

Preheat the oven to 350 degrees. Line muffin tins with paper liners.

In a small bowl, sift together the flour, cocoa powder, baking powder, baking soda, and salt. In a large measuring cup, combine the buttermilk, food coloring, vinegar, and vanilla.

In the bowl of an electric mixer fitted with the paddle attachment, beat the butter and sugar on medium speed for 1 minute, until light. Add the eggs, one at a time, and beat until combined. With the mixer on low speed, add the dry ingredients and the wet ingredients alternately in 3 parts, beginning and ending with the dry ingredients, and mix until combined. Stir with a rubber spatula to be sure the batter is mixed.

Scoop the batter into the muffin cups with a 2¼-inch ice cream scoop or large spoon. Bake for 25 to 30 minutes, until a toothpick inserted in the centers comes out clean. Cool completely in the pans and frost the cupcakes with Red Velvet Frosting.

red velvet frosting

8 ounces	cream cheese, at room temperature
12 tablespoons	(1½ sticks) unsalted butter, at room temperature
½ teaspoon	pure vanilla extract
3½ cups	sifted confectioners' sugar (¾ pound)

Place the cream cheese, butter, and vanilla in the bowl of an electric mixer fitted with the paddle attachment, and mix on medium speed just until combined. Don't whip! Add the sugar and mix until smooth.

rum raisin tiramisù

SERVES 8

Tiramisù is delicious and so easy to make; I thought, there must be another flavor besides the classic espresso and rum. I adore rum raisin ice cream, and Rum Raisin Rice Pudding (Barefoot Contessa Family Style), so I decided to play around with rum raisin tiramisù. Other than heating the raisins with rum, there's no cooking at all! You can make this a day in advance, so it's a great dessert for a dinner party.

Mascarpone is an Italian cream cheese. If you can't find it in the grocery store, try an Italian specialty store. The imported ones are best.

¾ cup	raisins
1 cup	plus 2 tablespoons Mount Gay dark rum, divided
6	extra-large egg yolks, at room temperature
½ cup	sugar
16 to 18 ounces	Italian mascarpone cheese
¾ cup	freshly squeezed orange juice, divided (2 oranges)
1½ teaspoons	pure vanilla extract
	Seeds scraped from 1 vanilla bean
24 to 30	Italian ladyfingers or savoiardi cookies
	Shaved semisweet chocolate, for garnish

Place the raisins and 2 tablespoons of the rum in a bowl, cover with plastic wrap, and place in the microwave on high for 1 minute. Uncover and set aside to cool.

Beat the egg yolks and sugar in the bowl of an electric mixer fitted with the paddle attachment on high speed for 5 minutes, until very thick and light yellow. Lower the speed to low and mix in the mascarpone until smooth. With the mixer still on low, add ½ cup of the rum, ¼ cup of the orange juice, the vanilla extract, and the seeds from the vanilla bean. Stir until combined.

Pour the remaining ½ cup of rum and remaining ½ cup of orange juice in a shallow bowl. Dip each ladyfinger in the rum mixture and arrange them in one layer in a 9 × 12 × 2-inch rectangular or oval dish. Break a few of the ladyfingers in smaller pieces, dip them in the rum mixture, and fill the spaces. Sprinkle half the rum-soaked raisins on top. Pour half the mascarpone mixture over and spread evenly. Add a second layer of dipped ladyfingers, rum-soaked raisins, and mascarpone mixture. Smooth the top, cover with plastic wrap, and refrigerate for at least 6 hours, but preferably overnight.

Sprinkle the top with the shaved chocolate and serve cold.

If you're worried about eating raw eggs, choose another dessert. You can't make tiramisù without using raw eggs.

old-fashioned banana cake

SERVES 8

At Barefoot Contessa we always seemed to have too many overripe bananas so I came up with this delicious banana cake to use them up. Eventually, the cake was so popular that we didn't have enough bananas to meet the demand for the cake!

If you need to get eggs to room temperature quickly, put them in a bowl of warm water for 5 minutes.

3	very ripe bananas, mashed
¾ cup	granulated sugar
½ cup	light brown sugar, lightly packed
½ cup	vegetable oil
2	extra-large eggs, at room temperature
½ cup	sour cream
1 teaspoon	pure vanilla extract
	Grated zest of 1 orange
2 cups	all-purpose flour
1 teaspoon	baking soda
½ teaspoon	kosher salt
½ cup	coarsely chopped walnuts
	Cream Cheese Frosting (recipe follows)
	Walnut halves, for decorating

Preheat the oven to 350 degrees. Grease and flour a 9 × 2-inch round cake pan.

In the bowl of an electric mixer fitted with the paddle attachment, mix the bananas, granulated sugar, and brown sugar on low speed until combined. With the mixer still on low, add the oil, eggs, sour cream, vanilla, and orange zest. Mix until smooth.

In a separate bowl, sift together the flour, baking soda, and salt. With the mixer on low, add the dry ingredients and mix just until combined. Stir in the chopped walnuts. Pour the batter into the prepared pan and bake for 45 to 50 minutes, until a toothpick inserted in the center comes out clean. Cool in the pan for 15 minutes, turn out onto a cooling rack, and cool completely.

Spread the frosting thickly on the top of the cake and decorate with walnut halves.

cream cheese frosting

FOR ONE 9-INCH CAKE

6 ounces	cream cheese, at room temperature
6 tablespoons	(¾ stick) unsalted butter, at room temperature
1 teaspoon	pure vanilla extract
2½ cups	sifted confectioners' sugar (½ pound)

Mix the cream cheese, butter, and vanilla in the bowl of an electric mixer fitted with the paddle attachment on low speed until just combined. Don't whip! Add the sugar and mix until smooth.

strawberry shortcakes, deconstructed

SERVES 6

I had dinner recently at Taste, one of my favorite restaurants in New York City. For dessert, we ordered what turned out to be a deconstructed strawberry shortcake, which is so clever: lots of fresh strawberries marinated to give them the most flavor and little shortcake biscuits like cookies to eat with it. What a good idea!

2 cups	all-purpose flour
	Granulated sugar
1 tablespoon	baking powder
1 teaspoon	kosher salt
12 tablespoons	(1½ sticks) cold unsalted butter, diced
2	extra-large eggs, lightly beaten
½ cup	cold heavy cream
1	egg beaten with 2 tablespoons water or milk, for egg wash
2 pints	fresh strawberries, hulled and thickly sliced
2 tablespoons	Grand Marnier liqueur
	Sweetened whipped cream (see note)

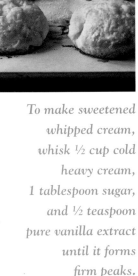

To make sweetened whipped cream, whisk ½ cup cold heavy cream, 1 tablespoon sugar, and ½ teaspoon pure vanilla extract until it forms firm peaks.

If you overwhip cream, just add a little extra cream and whisk it in.

Preheat the oven to 400 degrees. Line a sheet pan with parchment paper.

Sift the flour, 2 tablespoons sugar, the baking powder, and salt into the bowl of an electric mixer fitted with the paddle attachment. Add the butter and mix on low speed until the butter is the size of peas. Combine the eggs and heavy cream in a measuring cup and, with the mixer still on low, add to the flour mixture. Mix until just combined. The dough will be sticky.

Dump the dough out onto a well-floured surface. Flour a rolling pin and roll the dough ½ to ⅝ inch thick. You should see lumps of butter in the dough. Dip a 2-inch plain round cutter in flour and cut 16 to 18 biscuits. Place on the sheet pan, brush the tops of the biscuits with the egg wash, and sprinkle with sugar. Bake for 15 to

20 minutes, until the tops are browned and the insides are fully baked. Cool on the pan.

To serve, toss the strawberries with ⅓ cup of sugar and the Grand Marnier in a medium bowl. Place the berries in 6 martini glasses, top each with a dollop of whipped cream, and serve with 2 or 3 shortcakes on the side.

ultimate peach ice cream

MAKES 2 QUARTS

I've struggled for years to make peach ice cream—one that tastes like ripe peaches and cream. Almost every recipe is flavored with almond extract, which competes with the delicate peach flavor. Instead, I tried peaches, Sauternes, and Grand Marnier and came up with the perfect balance. I chill the mixture and pour it into the ice cream maker when we sit down to dinner so the ice cream is the right consistency when we're ready for dessert.

4	large ripe peaches (about 1½ pounds)
1½ cups	sugar, divided
½ cup	Sauternes
2 tablespoons	Grand Marnier liqueur
2 tablespoons	freshly squeezed lemon juice
2 teaspoons	pure vanilla extract
10	extra-large egg yolks
3 cups	half-and-half
1 cup	heavy cream
¼ teaspoon	kosher salt

Bring a large saucepan of water to a boil, add the peaches, and simmer for 30 seconds, until the skins loosen. Use a slotted spoon to transfer the peaches to a bowl of cool water. Peel the peaches, discard the pits, and place the fruit in a food processor fitted with the steel blade. Add ½ cup of the sugar, the Sauternes, Grand Marnier, lemon juice, and vanilla. Purée and set aside.

In a medium saucepan, whisk together the remaining 1 cup sugar, the yolks, half-and-half, cream, and salt. Cook over medium-low heat for 5 to 10 minutes, stirring constantly with a wooden spoon, until the mixture begins to thicken (it will register 180 degrees on a thermometer) and thickly coats the back of the spoon. Immediately pour through a sieve into a bowl.

Stir the peach purée into the custard, transfer it to sealed containers, and refrigerate until very cold. Freeze in batches in an ice cream machine according to the manufacturer's directions. Serve immediately or freeze in containers and soften before serving.

chocolate hazelnut cookies

MAKES 18 SANDWICH COOKIES

This is another variation of my friend Eli Zabar's delicious shortbread cookies. I love the combination of shortbread, roasted hazelnuts, and chocolate. The shortbread can be baked in advance, wrapped with plastic, and then filled with Nutella just before serving.

½ cup	whole hazelnuts
¾ pound	(3 sticks) unsalted butter, at room temperature
1 cup	granulated sugar
1 teaspoon	pure vanilla extract
1 teaspoon	pure almond extract
3½ cups	all-purpose flour
½ teaspoon	kosher salt
¾ cup	chocolate hazelnut spread, such as Nutella
	Confectioners' sugar, for dusting

Preheat the oven to 350 degrees.

Place the hazelnuts on a sheet pan, roast for 10 minutes, and allow to cool. Place the nuts in the bowl of a food processor fitted with the steel blade and pulse until finely ground.

Meanwhile, in the bowl of an electric mixer fitted with the paddle attachment, mix the butter and granulated sugar together on low speed until they are just combined. Stir in the vanilla and almond extracts plus 2 teaspoons of water. In a medium bowl, sift together the flour and salt and then, with the mixer on low, add it slowly to the butter mixture. Add the hazelnuts and mix on low until the dough comes together. Dump onto a floured board and shape into a disk. Wrap in plastic and chill for 30 minutes.

On a floured board, cut the dough in half and roll each piece ¼ inch thick. (Be sure it's not thicker.) Cut 36 (2¾-inch) rounds with a plain or fluted cutter. Use a ¾-inch cutter to cut a small circle out of the middle of half the cookies. Place all the cookies on sheet pans lined with parchment paper and chill for 15 minutes.

Bake for 20 to 25 minutes, rotating once, until the edges of the cookies begin to brown. Allow to cool to room temperature.

Spread the Nutella thickly on the flat side of each solid cookie. Dust the tops of the cutout cookies lightly with confectioners' sugar and place them on top of the Nutella, dusted side up.

new york egg cream

FOR EACH SERVING

It doesn't have eggs and it usually doesn't even have cream, but it sure is delicious. Classically an egg cream was made with seltzer from a siphon—the kind of bottle with a lever at the top—but club soda from the grocery store will do just fine. This is a classic Eastern European drink that came with Jewish immigrants to the Lower East Side of New York. Fox's U-Bet chocolate syrup is essential.

Fox's U-Bet chocolate flavor syrup
Cold whole milk or half-and-half
Ice-cold club soda or seltzer water

Pour 3 tablespoons of chocolate syrup and ¼ cup of milk or half-and-half into a 16-ounce glass. While beating vigorously with a fork, slowly add club soda until the glass is almost full. Add a straw and serve very cold.

fleur de sel caramels

MAKES 16 CARAMELS

Each time I tested this recipe, my friends ate all the caramels—no one even seemed to care that they weren't perfect. I serve them with coffee after dinner or pack them in glassine bags with ribbons for hostess gifts.

	Vegetable oil
1½ cups	sugar
¼ cup	light corn syrup
1 cup	heavy cream
5 tablespoons	unsalted butter
1 teaspoon	fine fleur de sel, plus extra for sprinkling
½ teaspoon	pure vanilla extract

It's easier to cut the caramels if you brush the knife with flavorless oil like corn oil.

Line an 8-inch square baking pan with parchment paper, allowing it to drape over 2 sides, then brush the paper lightly with oil.

In a deep saucepan (6 inches wide and 4½ inches deep), combine ¼ cup water, the sugar, and corn syrup and bring them to a boil over medium-high heat. Boil until the mixture is a warm golden brown. Don't stir—just swirl the pan. Watch carefully, as it can burn quickly at the end!

In the meantime, in a small pot, bring the cream, butter, and 1 teaspoon of fleur de sel to a simmer over medium heat. Turn off the heat and set aside.

When the sugar mixture is done, turn off the heat and slowly add the cream mixture to the sugar mixture. Be careful—it will bubble up violently. Stir in the vanilla with a wooden spoon and cook over medium-low heat for about 10 minutes, until the mixture reaches 248 degrees (firm ball) on a candy thermometer. Very carefully (it's hot!) pour the caramel into the prepared pan and refrigerate for a few hours, until firm.

When the caramels are cold, pry the sheet from the pan onto a cutting board. Cut the square in half. Starting with a long side, roll one piece of the caramel up tightly into an 8-inch-long log. Repeat with the second piece. Sprinkle both logs with fleur de sel, trim the ends, and cut each log in 8 pieces. Cut glassine or parchment paper into 4 × 5-inch pieces and wrap each caramel individually, twisting the ends. Store in the refrigerator and serve the caramels chilled.

white chocolate bark

MAKES 16 PIECES

Good vanilla is my favorite flavoring, which is why I love white chocolate. It's also a great base here for salty pistachios, tart cranberries, and sweet dried apricots. After dinner, when we move to the living room, I like to serve a little brandy, some white chocolate bark, and a bowl of clementines to continue the party.

½ cup	whole shelled salted pistachios
16 ounces	good white chocolate, finely chopped (see note)
¼ cup	dried cranberries
¼ cup	medium-diced dried apricots

Preheat the oven to 350 degrees. Using a pencil, draw an 8 × 10-inch rectangle on a piece of parchment paper. Turn the parchment paper over so the pencil mark doesn't get onto the chocolate and place it on a sheet pan.

Place the pistachios in one layer on another sheet pan and bake for 8 minutes. Set aside to cool.

Place three quarters of the white chocolate in a heat-proof glass bowl and put it in the microwave on high for 30 seconds. (Time it with your watch for accuracy.) Stir the chocolate with a rubber spatula, return it to the microwave for another 30 seconds, then stir again. Continue to heat and stir in 30-second intervals until the chocolate is *just* melted. Immediately stir in the remaining chocolate and allow it to sit at room temperature, stirring often, until it's completely smooth. (If you need to heat it a little more, place it in the microwave for another 15 seconds.)

Pour the melted chocolate onto the parchment paper and spread it lightly to fill the drawn rectangle. Sprinkle the top evenly with the cooled pistachios, the cranberries, and apricots. Press the nuts and fruit lightly so they will set in the chocolate. Set aside for at least 2 hours until firm or refrigerate for 20 minutes. Cut or break the bark in 16 pieces and serve at room temperature.

Be sure to use very good white chocolate (not chips) such as Callebaut or Valrhona. They are available at specialty food stores.

more easy tips!

Chinese take-out containers for picnics

17

Flat platters

18

French bread baskets

19

Gel mats

20

Large basket for Trays

21

Cast-iron skillets

22

2 dishwashers

23

Sharp Knives

24

All·Clad pots

25

White bake ware

26

Extra Cuisinart bowl

27

PepperMate peppermill

28

Large stockpot

29 Lots of timers

30 Lots of sheet pans

31 Grocery pads

32 Parchment paper for baking pans

33

Lots of measures

34

thermometers

35

Counting ingredients

36

Ice cream scoops

37 Crocks w/ utensils

38 Pop. up sponges

39 Lemons + limes on the counter

40 Salt crock

41

spoons + spatulas

42

Candy thermometer

43

White towels

44

Tasting spoons

45 Lots of white plates

46 dish towels for napkins

47 Big bowl to chill wine

48 Lots of white platters

49   Pretty dessert plates

50   Glasses for vases

51   Placecards

52   unironed napkins

53

54

Chinese strainer

Box grater

55

56

coffee grinder for spices

Salad spinner

57

Kitchen twine

58

vegetable peelers

59

professional utensils

60

rasp zester

61

Pro plastic wrap

62

Mise en place

63

French rolling pin

64

Cooking scale

65 Salad bowl

66 Storage Containers

67 Graduated bowls

68 Pastry bags

index